Win Your First Year in Teacher Leadership

Feel empowered during your first year as a team or department leader by applying the concise tips and tools in this book.

Author Stephen Katzel shows you how to create an effective system to integrate into a new leadership team, create meaningful professional development, facilitate parent conferences, coach teachers, interview for your next role, handle difficult situations, and more!

Perfect for beginning leaders, the book's examples, anecdotes, and practical tools are quick and easy to implement and will help you get off to a strong start on your leadership journey, where you can broaden your impact beyond the classroom and help others succeed.

Stephen Katzel lives in Rockville, Maryland, located right outside of Washington D.C. He is currently an administrator but has served as a team leader, department chair, and middle school social studies teacher. He is also author of *Win Your First Year of Teaching Middle School: Strategies and Tools for Success*.

T0383447

Win Your First Year in Teacher Leadership

A Toolkit for Team Leaders and Department Chairs

Stephen Katzel

Routledge
Taylor & Francis Group

NEW YORK AND LONDON

Cover image: © Getty Images

First published 2022
by Routledge
605 Third Avenue, New York, NY 10158

and by Routledge
2 Park Square, Milton Park, Abingdon, Oxon, OX14 4RN

Routledge is an imprint of the Taylor & Francis Group, an informa business

© 2022 Stephen Katzel

The right of Stephen Katzel to be identified as author of this work has been asserted in accordance with sections 77 and 78 of the Copyright, Designs and Patents Act 1988.

Library of Congress Cataloging-in-Publication Data
A catalog record for this book has been requested

ISBN: 978-1-032-13643-1 (hbk)
ISBN: 978-1-032-12656-2 (pbk)
ISBN: 978-1-003-23027-4 (ebk)

DOI: 10.4324/9781003230274

Typeset in Palatino
by Apex CoVantage, LLC

Access the Support Material:
www.routledge.com/9781032126562

This book is humbly dedicated to all educators.

Contents

Acknowledgments

I am eternally grateful to my parents who have supported me in any endeavor I have pursued.

About the Author

Stephen Katzel lives in Rockville, Maryland, located right outside of Washington D.C. He is currently an administrator but has served as a team leader, department chair, and middle school social studies teacher. Along with writing, he enjoys hiking, playing baseball, running, and traveling the country. He is also author of *Win Your First Year of Teaching Middle School: Strategies and Tools for Success.*

Support Material

The tools available in this book also appear in the Appendix, for ease of photocopying. Additionally, they can be found on our website so you can easily print them for your own use. They can be found on the book product page here:

www.routledge.com/9781032126562.

Introduction

The purpose of this book is to provide practical advice and tips to educators in their first leadership position in the new digital age. Being a school-based leader presents unique challenges and opportunities for growth in a variety of ways. Whether you are a team leader or department chair, you will be presented opportunities to work with students, staff, and the community in different ways than before now that you have a leadership position. All your previous experience as an educator will serve as a foundation for you to begin your leadership journey. Transitioning to a leadership position is one of the most exciting moments in your career. However, it is important to transition into your first leadership position with a "winning system". Having a winning system for your leadership role is imperative because your scope of responsibilities is now much broader than it was before. Developing new and experienced teachers, running meetings, meeting with parents, establishing community outreach, and so many more things are expected of you once you step into that leadership role. The purpose of this book is to give you and all other leaders in the first-year, applicable strategies and advice that you can use on your first day and beyond. My goal is to empower every school leader with tools and methods to "win" their first year in leadership. The winning system I developed was a direct result of the challenges and opportunities I faced as a new leader earlier in my career. I started my first leadership position during my fifth year of teaching as a team leader. However, many educators find themselves in new leadership roles as early as their second year or later in their career. I strongly believe that it does not matter when you begin

DOI: 10.4324/9781003230274-1

your leadership journey, it matters how you begin your leadership journey. Developing a winning system in your first year as a new leader will set you up for success throughout your career.

Again, I have a strong belief that developing a winning system allows for first-year leaders to be successful regardless of any type of leadership position that they hold. This book encompasses all the systems and processes that I have developed over the years as a school-based leader. The emphasis of this book is to give you applicable actions and methods you can use to make the transition to your first leadership position easier. Throughout my career, I have enjoyed taking numerous classes on leadership development. While taking classes to learn about leadership are useful, applying what you learned with a department of fifteen people can be challenging. Implementing a winning system as a new leader will help you reach each staff member that you supervise.

I believe my perspective provides a fresh and unique outlook on education and how first-year leaders can adapt their own styles into my winning system. There were several factors that led me to write this book. As a new leader, I started my first leadership position two days before the year started during the pre-service week! I interviewed on Wednesday and accepted my first leadership position on Thursday. This meant I had three days to prepare for my new leadership position, while lesson planning for a new grade level. Over the weekend, I was scrambling to adjust to my new role and looked for resources to help with my transition to my new leadership role. Most resources I found on school-based leadership were hundreds of pages and overwhelming. I did not have the time or energy that weekend or during my first year as a leader to read through hundreds of pages of content. I value your time and did not want to write a long and formulaic book. Keeping these factors in mind, I was intentional in what topics are discussed in this book and as well as the length. Your time is valuable to me, and I intend for you to get something out of each page of this book.

Throughout the first year in my leadership role, I was extremely lucky and had the support of many gifted leaders. However, all those gifted leaders have limited time! There is always an extent to which other school leaders can meet with you. That is why I wanted to create this book – to give new leaders a "playbook" to refer to throughout their first year. It is also possible you may not be as lucky as I was. There may not be other leaders that want to help you in your first year. Regardless of this, my book will provide a clear system to help you adapt to your new leadership role. The advice I give is relevant, practical, centered around common sense, and focuses on using technology efficiently.

Success as a first-year leader can be measured in numerous ways and can vary by individual expectations. Success can be measured by how well you adapted to your new role, connections you made with students, connections you made with the community or connections you made with staff. In my opinion, being organized and utilizing technology will allow you to be successful as a new leader, regardless of what your definition of "success" looks like. Later, I delve into how to structure your winning system as a new leader. This will involve being hyper-organized, using technology efficiently, and having consistent routines with the staff members you supervise.

Your first year as a new leader will be exciting and full of surprises that you did not encounter previously. In my first year as a new leader. I felt similar to being a first-year teacher again! The situations I encountered were not unique to myself, and you will face very similar challenges as well. Whether the challenges are with fellow leaders in the building, staff members, community members, or students, leadership roles bring different obstacles than you encountered in the past. I had to get creative and take risks when dealing with all these new experiences. Again, I was lucky in the amount of support I received from fellow leaders in the building. However, there were many times where I could not seek advice for a variety of reasons. No matter what your circumstances are during your first leadership role, you must adapt and overcome them. Use this book as a guide to alleviate the pressure that will come with being a new leader. You are going to do an amazing job and this year will make you feel energized. Value the experiences you will have each day and you have in this role because you are a leader. You are going to "win" your first year of being a new leader!

1

Setting Up a Winning System

Congratulations on your new leadership position! All the experiences you have had in your career have culminated in a school trusting you to not only promote student achievement but adult achievement as well. Whether you are a team leader or department chair, you are now in a unique position to make a transformational change on a school-wide level. Developing a "winning system" for your new role as a school-based leader is imperative for your continued success as a school leader. My definition of a "winning system" does not come from a search engine or from a college textbook. I have developed a "winning system" for my leadership roles through extensive experiences as a school leader. There are numerous ways to develop a winning system as a school leader. What works for some may not work for others. However, there are always three commonalities in each winning system that school leaders develop. Organization, consistency, and adaptability are the three pillars to a "winning system" for leadership positions. Again, many school leaders will have variations of these three pillars, but they are all present in some capacity in successful leaders' systems. Without clear organization, it will be difficult to keep track of important documents and lead any department when things aren't accessible (I will talk more about this later). Without consistency, staff will always be unsure of what you expect from them as members of your team, department, or school. Without adaptability, leaders will have difficulty adjusting to rapid change

DOI: 10.4324/9781003230274-2

and expectations that occur frequently when you are a school leader. Regardless of how you approach the three pillars, the ultimate goal for each school leader is student achievement and staff achievement. Student and staff achievement are complexly intertwined, and school leaders must recognize this to best serve the students, staff, and community. Developing the abilities of staff members will directly lead to an increase in student achievement.

A closer look at the three pillars:

- **Organization** for school leaders is having a system to organize important documents, emails, meeting notes, and much more. If another school leader asks for training that you developed, can the school leader find it with ease? Can files from the previous school year be located within five minutes? If a staff member asks for meeting notes, could they be located and sent out with ease? Organization for school leaders is essentially the ability to maintain important documents in an efficient way.
- **Consistency** is being reliable and unchanging in how you communicate and structure your team or department. Do staff members know the days that you run team meetings? Do you send the weekly agenda out on the same day each week or a different day? Is each meeting structured in the same manner? Are the roles for staff members during meetings consistent? Consistency for school leaders is essentially the ability to be relied upon by students, staff, and the community.
- **Adaptability** is the ability for school leaders to change their mindset, strategies, and actions to promote student and adult achievement. Does the school leader handle change well? How does the school leader act in the face of adversity? How does the school leader respond when things do not go as planned? Is the school leader conducting the same types of professional development each month? Has the school leader taken risks in their leadership role? Has the school leader tried different approaches when working with students, staff, and the community? Adaptability for school leaders is essentially the ability to change approaches in the face of adversity and change.

Having a clear system of organization is the most important pillar in building your winning system. Now that you are in a leadership position, you will start receiving significantly more emails, meetings, and overall responsibilities.

I am going to delve into how to structure your personal calendar, files related to leadership, and how to structure your online homepage for staff members to access. The more organized that you are, the smoother your system runs. The smoother your system runs, the less stressed out you are! Being able to access important files with ease by school year and topic leads to you doing your job more effectively. Maintaining a clearly structured personal calendar aids in your ability to adapt to the new challenges of leadership.

Structuring Your Personal Calendar

Before embarking on my leadership journey, I never used a personal calendar and would always laugh when seeing colleagues walk around with a huge paper calendar or personal planner. When I refer to a personal calendar, I am talking about a planner that is bound and has all twelve months of the year. After getting my first leadership position, I quickly realized that using a personal (paper) calendar and a digital calendar completely optimized my work schedule and led me to be hyper-organized. I walked into my first meeting with other leaders in my school building with no calendar, paper, or pen. I sat through a 45-minute meeting typing notes into my cell phone and was struggling to keep up with my notes. As soon as that meeting ended, I immediately bought a personal calendar for each month of the school year. Using your cell phone's calendar effectively is intertwined with maintaining your personal calendar. I will circle back to this point later on.

Ensure that your personal calendar has all twelve months of the school year and make sure you do not share your personal planner with anyone. Regardless of your leadership role, you will be part of or lead numerous meetings related to students, teachers, other leaders, and the community. When leading meetings with parents and staff, you will encounter confidential information that you will write down in the meeting's notes. That is why is important to make sure your personal calendar stays confidential and for your eyes only. In addition to having notes from parents and staff, you will need to use the personal calendar to keep track of your schedule. Below exemplifies what my personal calendar looks like for the first month of school. I purposely left weekends blank because each weekend varies for me. Another important thing to mention is to choose one school-related email and calendar to work from. Many school districts will offer two email addresses that serve different purposes for each employee. My recommendation would be to type into a search engine "How to forward all emails to one specific email address". This will allow you to only have to check one email account and one calendar each day. I also recommend choosing an email address that has cloud storage so that you can have all your files located in one area as well. Keeping all your important emails, dates, and files in one location will make you significantly more organized than a person who has multiple email addresses and multiple calendars to check. I have heard of colleagues in the past missing extremely important emails or calendar invites because they were juggling multiple email addresses. In my first year of teaching, I was wasting time each day checking two email accounts and two calendars. I know this may seem trivial, but the saved time adds up over the course of the year.

Monday	Tuesday	Wednesday	Thursday	Friday
August 2	August 3	August 4	August 5	August 6
1.Pre-Send an email to Mr. Doe about formal observation	1. Send email with data collection form for "Kid Talk"	1. Analyze Kid Talk data before the meeting	1. Team Meeting during fourth period	1. Send out weekly agenda to staff for upcoming week
2. Observe 7th Grade Science	2. Meet with other department leaders for upcoming visit for high school enrollment	2. Team Meeting during fourth period	2. Draft weekly agenda for the week of August 9	2. Parent-Teacher Conference at 12:00 for Student John Doe
3. Send feedback to observed teacher	3. Analyze most recent state test scores for Math	3. Observe Seventh Grade Social Studies Cohort	3. Leadership Meeting at 4 pm	3. Cheek observation schedule for following week
4. Sync events to cell phone calendar	4. Sync events to cell phone calendar	4. Sync events to cell phone calendar	4. Sync events to cell phone calendar	4. Sync events to cell phone calendar

Figure 1.1 Personal Calendar- August 20XX

In addition to having a paper calendar, I add each event or task in my phone's calendar as well. I ensure that each day I update my cell phone's calendar to match my "paper calendar". After I input each event, I always ensure there is a reminder on for my phone to buzz, so that I am reminded to complete the task. I always have my cell phone in my pocket, and this allows me to be reminded of tasks while I am on the move. Realistically, you won't be able to carry your calendar with you the entirety of the day, so having your phone helps keep you organized in this regard. Some folks may say having a digital and paper calendar that is identical may be "too much" work and tedious. However, using my two-calendar system consistently and effectively has allowed me to be hyper-organized and not miss any meetings, forget about tasks, or miss any scheduled observations. For example, I have a weekly reminder in my calendar that goes off at approximately 8:15 am each Monday morning to send out a data collection form to my team. I set the reminder on my phone to be during the first five minutes of my planning period to ensure that I will be able to send it out, before potentially getting pulled into another meeting. I also put reminders on my phone for after-school meetings, reminders to observe teachers, and much more. The phone calendar events do not need to be written in detail. Below is an example of a simple reminder, that allows me to remember an event and stay organized. Again, when you're a leader, there will be so many different things you must keep up with. Having a clear system of organization enables you to keep up with everything with greater ease than leaders who do not have a system or organization.

Figure 1.2 Meeting reminder

Organizing Your Digital Folders for Success

Having all your team, department, and leadership files organized effectively will allow you to access needed documents with ease. Having structures implemented consistently each year will enable you to access templates from previous years so that you are not always starting from scratch. Not only will having digital folders organized intentionally enhance your own organization, but it will enhance your leadership. Having files and important documents available in the cloud will allow staff members that you supervise to be more organized as well. School districts have different companies that they work with for cloud storage. However, each cloud storage provider enables you to share folders and documents with others. With technology becoming increasingly prevalent in education, it is imperative for educational leaders to utilize technology with their students and staff. One of my favorite sayings is "Don't work for technology, make technology work for you". Effectively implementing a system of organization will allow technology to "work for you". Later in this chapter, I will show you examples of how shared documents and folders will further enhance your leadership capabilities.

Organize Your Files, Maximize Your Leadership

Organization is the first pillar of developing a winning system for your leadership role for a variety of reasons. The first few days of my leadership journey involved organizing years upon years of files that my predecessors had developed over the course of the past decade. It was extremely time-consuming looking through all the old files and organizing them by topic and year. However, since I spent time organizing the files, I was then able to have a better grasp on what was expected of me, what the team did in the past, and how things were structured over the last decade. The system I developed personally fits my organizational system and allows me to find files with ease. The system can be implemented for a school team or department. By implementing a winning system for organization, you will be able to maximize your leadership capabilities and manage your time effectively in comparison to a disorganized leader. Another benefit of having a clear organizational system is the ability to share important documents with your staff.

⟨ ⟩ **8th Grade Team**

8th Grade Graduation

8th Grade Homerooms

8th Grade Mentori...Program

8th Grade Orientation

9th Grade Parent Night

Academic Interventions

Celebrations

Cohort Planning

Distance Learning

First Week of School

Hall Passes

Honor Roll

Meeting Agendas

Meetings

Parent Conferences

State Testing

Student of the Week

Supply List

Surveys

Weekly Student Analysis...d Social

Figure 1.3 Folders that contain important files and resources for a team leader.

Constructing and clearly organizing your files for a team that you supervise is imperative to successful management. If you are a team leader or in a similar role, you will have numerous roles and responsibilities in addition to teaching classes. Having a file for "meeting agendas" allows a team leader to keep track of what was discussed in the team meetings throughout the entire school year. On a side note, I would highly recommend sending out a weekly agenda to the team that you supervise, but I will delve into this further later. Keeping track of topics that were discussed in team meetings allows a team leader to not do too many of the same professional developments or cover similar topics repeatedly. As a team leader, you will work very closely with the school's administration and counseling department. From my experience, it is a good idea to share all your files with them as well, so that everyone is on the same page. Most cloud services have the option to share all your files, but not allow anyone to edit them. I highly recommend not letting anyone be able to edit your files because they may alter or delete things that are important. When I was in my third year as a leader, I shared files with a person who accidentally deleted half of my files! A tragedy was avoided because I backed up all my files on a flash drive. Had I not done this; all my hard work would have gone to waste due to a mistake by a colleague. Having a clear system of organization for your team's files will allow you to spend more time on other things related to the job. Leadership positions require a significant amount of organization to be efficient. Over the years, files may pile up and some leaders do not take the time to maintain their organizational system. A solution to this is seen below in an exemplified file for "8th Grade Homerooms". At the end of each school year, I add in a file for the specific year that I just completed. By adding in folders for specific years, I am furthering my organizational system and saving myself time down the road. If I ever get stuck on how to construct a specific document or training, I always look back on previous years' work to have something to go off. Adding different years into my organizational system allows me to not have to look at hundreds of files at the same time. It clears up the screen and enables me to find files more easily than if I keep everything in one folder without any designation on the year that the file was created.

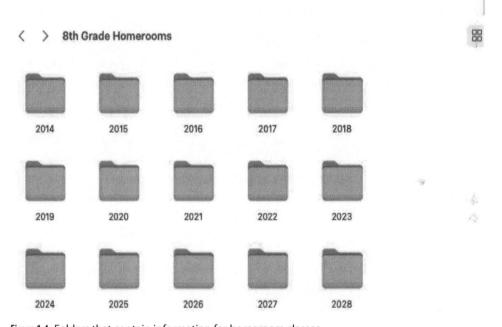

Figure 1.4 Folders that contain information for homeroom classes.

The Importance of Weekly Agendas

I highly recommend sending out a weekly team agenda each Friday before the start of the next school week. Having this consistency will deter teachers from asking "Are we meeting next week?" since they know that each Friday, they will obtain this information. Sending out weekly agendas to all teachers in the grade level that you supervise furthers your impact as a leader. Due to scheduling constraints and other factors, there is almost a zero percent chance that all teachers who teach a specific grade level can all attend the team meetings for that specific grade level. I will give an example to clarify my previous statement. At Stephen Katzel Middle School, all sixth grade team meetings occur during the fourth period. However, sixth-grade students have their elective classes during fourth period, which means that all arts, physical education, and music teachers cannot make the sixth grade team meetings due to the schedule. Although some teachers may not be able to attend the team meetings, it is important to include all the teachers in the weekly email that includes the agenda. Also, sending out a weekly team agenda allows team members to plan accordingly so that they can ideally attend each meeting in case they need to schedule any appointments for themselves or family members during the workday. I also made it a point to include the counseling department, other grade-level team leaders, the grade-level administrator, and principal in each weekly agenda email. This allows other leaders in the building to know what is occurring in my team and attend any meeting if they choose to do so. Below is an example of a weekly agenda that you could send out to your team each week. You can make the agenda as plain or elaborate as you would like. I personally recommend putting the room number and time of the meeting each week in case there are new staff members throughout the year. Including important dates on the team agenda allows team members to plan ahead and be reminded of important deadlines that are coming up. Also, I always include the topic that is being covered in the meeting, in order for team members to prepare for the team meeting. As a team leader, you should make every effort to keep the schedule consistent if you can. Most days off from school occur on a Monday, so I always tried to not schedule any meetings on a Monday unless necessary. Also, I tried avoiding scheduling meetings on Friday, since that is a popular day for personal leave. However, on Mondays and Fridays, the expectation for teachers was to meet with their colleagues that taught the same subject matter to plan. Essentially, Mondays and Fridays were an extra planning period for teachers. I strongly advise not scheduling meetings all five days of the workweek unless you really have to. Giving extra time for planning and collaboration helps teachers manage their workload. This also shows that you care about the team that you supervise and do not just schedule meetings for the sake of meeting. Another aspect of the schedule I would recommend keeping consistent is the days that you have discussions about students, implement professional development, and analyze data. For example, every Tuesday, the seventh grade team knows that they will be conducting a student analysis. Every Wednesday, the seventh grade team knows that professional development will occur in the team meeting. Students always crave structure, but so do adults. Adults do not want to always be guessing what the meetings they have to attend will be about. Another aspect of the meeting agenda is assigning roles for all of the meetings for that specific week. To keep meetings on track and to further engage team members, I highly recommend assigning roles to team members. Having team members keep track of time, take notes, and ensure that the group is on-task will ideally lead to more efficient team meetings. All three of the roles should be assigned on a rotating basis each week. Another aspect of team meetings that are worth mentioning: please start meetings on time and end the meetings on time as well. Staff members will dread coming to your meetings if they always start or end late. Staying consistent with the start and end times adds to your credibility as well.

<u>6th Grade Team Weekly Agenda</u>

School Logo

<u>Team Meeting Information – Room XXX from 2:00–2:30</u>

Monday 3/15	Tuesday 3/16	Wednesday 3/17	Thursday 3/18	Friday 3/19
No Team Meeting – Content Area Planning	Team Meeting – Student Analysis	Team Meeting – Professional Development	Team Meeting – Data Analysis	No Team Meeting – Content Area Planning

Important Dates:

1. 3/23 – Professional Day for Teachers
2. 3/30 – Progress Reports are due at 3:00
3. 4/1 – Start of Spring Break
4. 4/10 – End of the marking period

Roles:

1. Timekeeper –
2. Task Manager –
3. Notetaker –

Figure 1.5 Team Agenda

Weekly Student Analysis – Maintaining a Positive Team Culture

Having weekly discussions about students during team meetings is important for maintaining a positive team culture and school culture. Team meetings centered on student data can be implemented in different formats. One format that I was exposed to involved sending a data form each week to teachers to nominate students to discuss. Teachers would fill out the form and then I would choose which students to discuss based on teacher nominations. Then I would send out a data form for teachers to fill out about 2–3 specific students. I always put in the email "Only fill out the form if you teach any of the students below". The reason why I added this into each email was that I found myself getting many emails each week from the teacher stating, "I do not teach that student". This brings me to my next point: I always send out the forms to every teacher for that specific grade level in order to be more efficient with my time. Making email distribution lists that include <u>every</u> teacher that teaches a specific grade level saves time. For example, if I am the sixth grade team leader, I would send out the data forms to every sixth grade teacher, instead of individualized emails for specific data forms. Pulling the schedules of the students that you will discuss in the team meeting is time-consuming and honestly a waste of time. I always sent out the forms a week early to give myself time to gather data and to give teachers time to fill out the data. Below are examples of emails I would send to my team members using this type of student analysis format. I specifically worded both emails to make it clear who should fill out the forms and who should not fill out the forms. I also included clear due dates for submitting names and for filling out the forms. This is to avoid getting emails asking about when things are due. I would recommend copying and pasting both emails for the entirety of the year to keep your formatting and wording consistent. After teachers fill out the form to collect data on each student, you will print out the teacher data and distribute it to your team. In the "Student Analysis Team Meeting", each team member will receive a copy of the data and have a discussion on possible interventions and steps that can be taken to help the students discussed. Below is an example of what to include in the data collection form that can be sent out to teachers for "Student Analysis Team Meetings". I put a few general questions on the example data form. You can have the form be as descriptive or broad as you would like. I would recommend asking specific questions to get direct answers from teachers. Also, the team leader should be facilitating this discussion and actively engaged. I would recommend having another teacher take notes about purposed interventions and the next steps. Also, please note that even if a teacher does not teach any of the students that are brought up in the data analysis, they should be required to attend the team meeting and contribute to the student discussion. Student schedules can change, but either way, all students are "our students" regardless of who teaches them.

INITIAL EMAIL

Eighth grade teachers,

Please email me any student names that you would like to be brought up for our data discussion by 9:00 am on March 17th. This will be for our team meeting on March 24th.

Please include any information you would like to share about this student's academic or social progress.

Thank You,

Mr. Katzel

Data Collection Email

Eighth grade teachers,

If you teach any of the students listed below, please complete the data analysis form by 9:00 am on March 21st. We will have our data analysis meeting on March 24th.

If you teach more than one of the students below, you will have to fill out the form multiple times. If you do not teach any of the students listed below, you do not need to fill out the form.

Names:

Link to Form:

Thank You,

Mr. Katzel

Example Questions – Data Form

Teacher Name/Subject –

Student Name/Period –

Parent/Guardian Email(s) –

List any contact with parents/guardians –

Current Grade –

Have you used any interventions?

What ideas or next steps should be taken with this student?

Another student analysis format that I have been exposed to involves a completely different process than the one I described above. Each week, the grade-level team leader would meet with the grade-level administrator to identify students to discuss during a "Student Analysis Team Meeting". After this meeting, the team leader would put together a profile of 2–3 students to be discussed at the meeting. For example, all the students' grades, attendance, parent/guardian communication, test scores, and etc. When teachers come into the meeting, all of this data will be projected on the board for teachers to see. However, the twist to this format is that the team leader does not share with the team the names of the students that they are analyzing until after the data is discussed and interventions are proposed. The reasoning behind this is for staff to be more engaged in the meeting and to not bring in any personal biases about the student while discussing the data. I personally would only recommend using this method sparingly, because it takes longer than the previously mentioned method due to the "revealing of students" at the end of the meeting. Also, I have noticed that this format leads to more "deficit wording" in some scenarios. When I mention "deficit wording" it essentially means that someone is using words that put a student down rather than lift them up. Wording can be everything in how teachers view students and analyze data. For example, if I stated, "John Doe is awful at Algebra and has had a failing grade all year". After hearing that, you would think of negative aspects of John Doe's math ability. If I worded it like this, "John Doe has struggled in Algebra this year and his grades have not been where they should be. Let's think of interventions and strategies to help him". This statement presents a completely different view of the student and promotes solutions to problems. Too many times, problems are brought up to leadership without any solutions. Whenever I have brought up any problems with bosses, I always ensure I have solutions included as well. Not only does this make me not seem like a "complainer", but it also shows that I am actively looking for solutions.

Effectively Managing and Organizing a Department

As the leader of a content-specific department, you will have numerous responsibilities involving students, staff, and the community at large. Maintaining an effective organizational system will be imperative to your lasting success in the department chair role. The first thing you have to create are two folders to house all of your files. One folder will contain all of your files that are related to observing teachers formally and informally. Do not share this folder with your department because it is confidential information. The second folder will contain important information for your department and should be shared with each member. Most school districts will pay for some sort of cloud service, so you should share the folder with all members through whichever cloud service is available to you. Inside of the "Department Folder", you should have two of the same folders for each grade level that you supervise. In the example below, you can clearly see that sixth, seventh, and eighth-grade cohorts have separate folders for planning calendars and common tasks. As a department chair, it is extremely important that you have the quarterly planning calendars from each member of your department. This allows you to stay better organized and helps you keep track of the pace that teachers and cohorts are keeping. It is important to note that all teachers in specific cohorts should have the same planning schedule to ensure that each student is receiving the same content, regardless of the teacher. For example, you decided to do an unannounced observation for all three staff members that teach sixth grade social studies, you can check the day on the quarterly planning calendar to see what topic they are teaching that day. If all three teachers are on the same topic or lesson, you know that the cohort is on schedule in delivering their content. If one cohort member is two days behind and the other two cohort members are on schedule, you know that one teacher is falling behind schedule. With this knowledge, you can reach out to the teacher and ask if they need help. I always recommend allowing all staff members in your department to see everyone's quarterly planning calendars and common task assessments. To further explain "common task" assignments, think of them to help grade-level cohorts plan cohesively. Each teacher has their own style and way of delivering content. However, it is important that grade-level cohorts are assessing students in similar ways. Requiring each grade-level cohort to give one "common task" a week allows you to help teachers plan more cohesively. Asking department members to upload the common task to a shared folder also allows you to keep track of what is occurring with your department. Allowing your whole department to see each other's common tasks builds collaboration among staff members and allows other grade levels to get new ideas from other department members. For example, the seventh-grade cohort came up with a very creative "Exit Ticket" format. After uploading the exit ticket, the sixth and eighth-grade cohorts can see what seventh grade created and make something similar if they choose to do so. Another aspect of the department folder is including all dates for department meetings, important presentations, and articles. This allows your department members to access prior training and information from earlier in the year. Inside the department folders for quarterly calendars and common tasks, I added another layer of organization by adding in places to put files by the year they were created and the specific quarter in which they were implemented. Again, this allows you and your department to be extremely organized and able to collaborate as a team.

Figure 1.6 Department Chair Folders

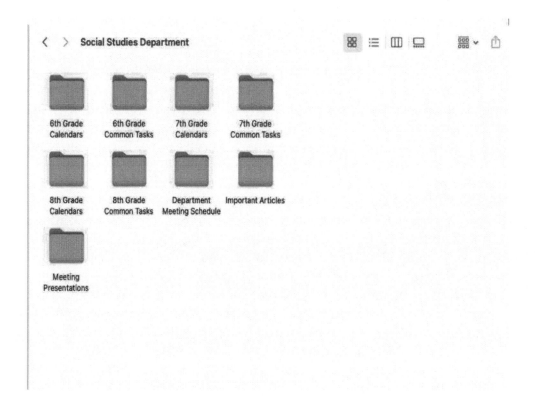

Figure 1.7 Example Social Studies Department Folders

⟨ ⟩   6th Grade Calendars

2018   2019   2020   2021

Figure 1.8 Example for Planning Calendars

⟨ ⟩   **6th Grade Common Tasks**

Quarter 1   Quarter 2   Quarter 3   Quarter 4

Figure 1.9 Example Folders for Common Tasks

When conducting formal and informal observations throughout the year, it is important to keep track of the date you observed the teacher and what you observed. I highly recommend having a form that you fill out each time you observe a teacher to maintain consistency and organization. I would include the date, learning objective, notes, and learning standards, and the amount of time you observed the lesson. Using an internet search engine, you can find hundreds of pre-made observation forms and checklists that other educators have made. You can make it as detailed or simple as you choose, but always take notes! Below is a way to keep track of your department's observations. Another tip I always give new department chairs is to send a follow-up email to whomever they observed within twenty-four hours. The email should include positive aspects of the observation and any potential next steps. For example, if you conducted a formal observation, you should give a time frame when your evaluation will be ready to be discussed. I would recommend having the "post-observation meeting" within two business days of your formal observation.

⟨ ⟩   **20XX-20XX Observations**

Observation Form   Teacher
& Checklist   Observa...Grid.pdf

Figure 1.10 Example Folders for a Department chair

Example Observation Grid

Name	Grade Level	Date	Formal Observation?	Informal Observation?
Mr. Katzel	Eighth Grade			

Name	Grade Level	Date	Formal Observation?	Informal Observation?
Mr. Doe	Sixth Grade			

When conducting department meetings, I would highly suggest making a meeting agenda. Some school districts want departments to meet once a week, three times a week, or once a month. Regardless of how often you meet, I would make an agenda to stay on track and be organized. Make sure to include roles for the meeting, such as timekeeper, notetaker, and task manager. I would use a variation of the "team leader" agenda that I talked about earlier. Team meetings and department meeting agendas can be similar in structure but obviously would contain different information. Whether it is a team meeting or a department meeting, I like to always allocate time for team or department members to share a new technological resource or lesson plan idea with the staff. Asking a staff member to create a ten-minute presentation will not only highlight their success but help other staff members learn a new skill. This builds the capacity of the presenter and of other team members. For example, school got moved online due to a once-in-a-generation event. I noticed that one staff member was very skilled at organizing their lesson plans in their online classroom. I would then ask that teacher in an email, "Good Evening, Mr. Doe, I noticed your amazing lesson plan structure online. Would you be able to present this to the team/department on 5/19? Thank you for your time, Stephen".

Another way to keep your department or team organized is to establish a protocol for naming and grading assignments. I highly recommend a rule for all your staff members to name and label their assignments with the same acronyms and to post them in the same location. I will start with the name of the assignments. Each teacher should label their assignments with a due date labeled as "DD" and a deadline labeled "DL". The due date is the day the assignment should be submitted for full credit. The deadline is the last day an assignment can be submitted for credit. An example of an assignment name with both acronyms could be, "12 Themes of Geography Assignment: DD – 5/17, DL – 5/24". Also, most school districts have an online portal where teachers can post their assignments and homework. I highly recommend requiring your department to upload homework and important classwork assignments on the online portal, so that everything is all in one location. This allows you to tell parents/guardians where all your team/department's assignments are with absolute certainty. If staff members struggle with uploading assignments, you can conduct a professional development session to help them. Having the due dates, deadlines, and assignments all in one location and consistent among your department will allow you to be more organized and allow you to answer any parent questions, should they come up in a meeting.

Addressing the "Technology Gap"

With regard to professional development, I want to briefly address the "tech gap" in education. Due to a variety of factors, many educators are hesitant to embrace technology in their classrooms. However, always say "Make technology work for you, do not work for technology". Building the capacity of your staff requires the implementation of technology into their classrooms. In the years I have spent as an educational leader, I have noticed a pattern of resistance in implementing educational technology into classrooms and I have made it a goal to help my staff members with technology. Whether it is making a short video or document that helps staff with technology, I always try to close the "technology gap". When you take on a leadership position, it is always important to focus on staff members' strengths and weaknesses. It is very possible that the staff you supervise does not have a "technology gap". Regardless of the ability level of your staff members, always encourage the use of technology to enhance the student and teacher experience.

Creating an "Email Bank"

As an instructional leader, you are going to be responsible for crafting hundreds of emails throughout the year. During my first year as a leader, I felt that I was dedicating a lot of time to crafting emails about a variety of topics that were well written, informative, and concise. After realizing how much time I was dedicating to crafting emails from scratch, I created an "email bank" to store emails that I wrote in the past and emails from staff members that I thought I could use down the line. I know it may seem tedious but saving important emails that I have written has saved me so much time over the last few years. Also, whenever I see a well-worded email from a staff member, I make sure to save it in my email bank, so that I have something to refer to in the future. In my email bank, I name the topic that the email covers, then I copy and paste the email I want to save inside the folder. I always ensure that my email bank is saved in my cloud for work so that I always have access to it. Below is an example of what an email bank can look like.

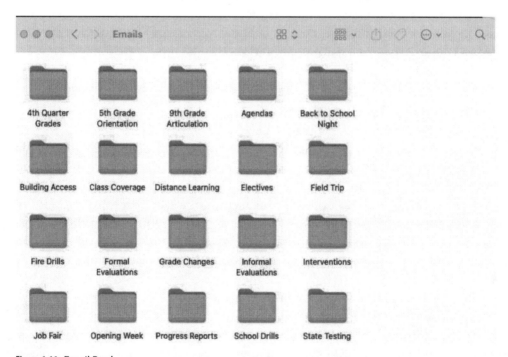

Figure 1.11 Email Bank

Final Thoughts

Everything that goes into being an effective school leader may seem overwhelming. But following these steps will help you develop a winning system and decrease your stress as the year goes on. The busiest month of my life was when I was establishing my winning system throughout the first month of my first leadership position and I was always working on my foundation. I use my winning system to this day since the three pillars are effective and applicable to all of the work I am involved in. Organization, consistency, and adaptability must be kept in mind when structuring your own winning system. Make sure that you stay consistent with your organizational systems and do not be afraid to take risks. Many people say that their worst year in education was their first year taking on a leadership position. I do not agree with that. Your mindset, preparation, and outlook will determine the success or lack of success during your first leadership position. Having a winning system will aid in achieving numerous successes throughout your first year and your career.

2

Integrating Into a Leadership Team and School

Unless you are starting your leadership position in a new school, there will be an established culture, staff dynamics, structures, and roles on the leadership team that you are joining. Each leadership team will have areas that they are excelling in and areas that can be improved upon. Navigating all the complexities of a leadership team on top of starting your new position can be challenging! In this chapter, I will discuss tips and ideas to implement to help smooth your transition to the new team and what actions to avoid to better integrate yourself into the position. By becoming aware of common missteps that other educators take when becoming integrated into a leadership team, you will be ready on your first day to sit in on a meeting and share your ideas with other leaders in the building. Remember the three pillars of a winning leadership system upon starting your new role: be organized, be consistent, and be adaptable throughout your first year and beyond. These three pillars will guide you through numerous situations and allow you to not only win your first year in a leadership position but every year after.

Introducing Yourself to the School

After accepting a leadership position there are going to be numerous things that you must do to complete the job effectively. However, before any of those tasks can be worked on and completed, you must introduce yourself to all your new colleagues. Regardless of if you were just hired as the new seventh

DOI: 10.4324/9781003230274-3

grade team leader or Social Studies department chair, introducing yourself to the entire staff is important to establish yourself as a member of the school community. There are going to be numerous instances where you are going to work with different staff members that are not in your grade level or subject matter. Whether that is helping a colleague in the hallway with a difficult situation, teaming up with a colleague during and after a school event, working with a colleague in a different grade level at a staff meeting, there are so many more instances will find yourself interacting and working with colleagues that you do not see on a daily basis. Below is an example of an email that you can write introducing yourself to staff members a few days after accepting your new leadership position.

Subject Line: 20XX-20XX School Year: Introduction

Good Afternoon,

My name is Stephen Katzel, and I am excited to be joining the amazing staff at John Doe Middle School as the Seventh Grade Team Leader. I am excited to make meaningful contributions to the school and community through collaboration with others. Please feel free to stop by my office during pre-service week to say hello. Have a great day!

Best,

Mr. Katzel

Introducing Yourself to the Leadership Team

I start almost every email that I send to a specific person or all staff members with "Good Morning", "Good Afternoon", or "Good Evening". The reason why I start emails in this "formal" manner is that I always feel that it is okay to be too formal in an email, but it is never okay to be too "informal" in an email. Starting off emails in this manner will also allow you to spend less time thinking about how you want to start an email. I always end emails with "Best" or "Thank You" to continue with my trend of being "formal" in my emails. I know you may be thinking, "These emails sound like a robot!" However, as time goes on, you will be able to use your own judgment on how you structure your emails to staff members. I highly recommend starting with a more formal tone for at least the first few months of your new position. As a new leader in a building, it will take time to develop relationships with staff members, and something as simple as how you structure your emails will aid in developing your relationships. By writing a "welcome email" to staff members, you can informally introduce yourself to a large group of people at once and extend an olive branch. Taking the time to personally introduce yourself to each staff member after you get hired is time-consuming and not doable when there are a hundred staff members! At a minimum, when staff members read your initial email, they will at least appreciate the effort you made to introduce yourself.

Limit the Number of Emails You Send Each Day

As a leader, there are so many things that happen in one school day! Communicating efficiently and effectively touches on all three pillars of a winning system. The number of emails that you send out each day should ideally be limited to two emails at most. Some days you may not send out an email to staff members and other days you may send out five due to circumstances in the school. However, do everything in your power to limit the number of emails that you send out to staff members to two per day. If you start sending too many emails out each day, staff members will either start to tune out your messages or skim them. This will lead to staff members missing out on important information that you are sending. In my opinion, the average educator would rather read one long email per day than receive five emails from the same person. Being concise in the emails that you write out to staff members is important as well. I have seen too many leaders in school buildings rant/ramble in their email messages to staff members that they are supervising. This leads to staff members becoming confused about the purpose and content of the message. To further expand on how staff members can become confused by an email, please ensure that the subject line of your email matches up with the content of your message. If you are sending an email about a meeting, your subject line should be similar to "4/15 Department Meeting". Including dates in the subject line of emails allows staff members to remember important dates with more ease as well. I always try to include dates in my emails for this reason.

Maintaining Email Etiquette

Maintaining "email etiquette" is another way to ensure that you are effectively communicating with staff members throughout your career. If you are ever sending a message to the entire school, please ensure that it is relevant to the entire school. I have seen too many educational leaders make the mistake of emailing the entire staff for no purpose. This leads me to my next point: please do not be the dreaded "reply all" staff member at your school! It is very frustrating to have a school leader send out an email to the entire staff and have the same 2–3 people always "reply all" instead of replying directly to the person. I know that this may seem silly to bring up, but I promise you the saying "less is more" goes a long way in terms of the number of emails that you send out on any given day. Another effective tip about sending emails is being mindful of the time of day you are communicating with staff members. I would recommend not sending emails out past 5:00 pm on a workday and to severely limit the number of emails you send to staff members over the week-end. Many educators have their work email on their phones and may start to get frustrated by seeing emails in the evening or on weekends, which leads to them to miss crucial information if they tune out your message. A way around this would be to schedule messages to be sent as a "scheduled send". Many email providers allow you to write out an entire email and schedule the time and date you would like for it to be sent. For example, today's date is Friday, January 15th and you have crafted an email reminding staff of a meeting on next Tuesday, January 19th. You can write the email on the 15th and have it sent to the recipients on the morning of the 19th. I would recommend utilizing the scheduled send feature of your email to allow you to be more organized and to promote a positive email etiquette.

Positive and Negative Emails

As a leader, you are going to encounter positive and negative emails from students, staff, and community members. Regardless of your role, I would highly recommend sending out one "positive email" per week about a staff member that you supervise. I would also recommend sending a positive email to the entire school. An example could be a picture from the lesson that you observed and 3–4 sentences as to why you were impressed with the lesson. Sending positive emails about other staff members helps to build a positive school culture and shows that you are recognizing staff members' accomplishments. Sending positive emails is a lot more fun than receiving nasty emails! However, as a leader, it is inevitable that you will receive less than friendly emails at times. Whenever I receive a nasty email, I ensure that I do not respond right away to avoid an "email war". An email war is when two or more parties engage in an argument over email that rarely leads to the issue at hand being solved. In the heat of the moment, I know it is difficult to not respond when someone is rude to you. Give yourself some time to answer them and possibly request a meeting with a third party to help. For example, say you are a team leader that just asked a staff member (Mr. John Doe) to send over data on a class you just observed in order to start writing up his observation report. Below is an example email exchange.

Subject Line: Post-Observation Data

Good Morning Mr. Doe,

Thank you for having me in your classroom last Monday. I really enjoyed your lesson on geography and know the students did too. I am starting to write up your observation report, could you send me the formative assessment data and class report so I can include the data in the report?

Thank You,

Mr. Katzel
Subject Line: RE: Post-Observation Data

Mr. Katzel,
I am not collecting this data at this time and I feel that you can look up the information on my class.

Subject Line: Post-Observation Meeting – 2/27 at 10:15 (Room 200)

CC: Mrs. Poe

Mr. Doe,
I understand your point of view, but I feel that this conversation should occur in a meeting and not over email, where things get lost in translation. I will set up a meeting with you, Mrs. Poe (Mr. Doe's department chair), and myself so we can problem-solve.

Thank You,

Mr. Katzel

Notice in my email reply, I was not aggressive and stated that I wanted to solve the issue at hand with a third party present. I did not engage with his rudeness and I put the meeting's information in the subject line so that he knew we would meet about this. Inviting a third party to attend the meeting is not a "gotcha"; it is a way to help guide a potentially difficult conversation with a staff member that you supervise. I would recommend inviting the department chair or team leader of the staff member that you are engaging with. This allows their direct supervisor to be privy to the situation but also allows you to have a third party present. I would recommend emailing the team leader or department chair separately to make them aware of the situation before including them in the email reply to the staff member. On the flip side, if you are a team leader or department chair in this situation, you could ask the administrator that supervises your department to be part of the meeting as well. Again, in the heat of the moment, it is very hard to have the self-control to not react to a rude email. However, you are an instructional leader in the building now and must always "be the bigger person". I know it is not easy and I have made mistakes in the past, but I am constantly learning and improving as a leader.

Serving on Committees and Being Assigned Non-Ideal Tasks

As a new leader in the building, you will have to build relationships and trust with all staff members throughout your first year. Most schools assign members of the leadership team to committees that oversee a variety of projects and initiatives at the school. For example, of the 18 members on a leadership team, four are assigned to creating and designing homeroom lessons for the entirety of the school year, while the remaining 14 members are assigned to other committees and tasks that require collaboration. As a new leader in my building, I was excited to dive headfirst into my committee and was extremely excited when I attended my first meeting. All my excitement was quickly wiped away when I was assigned to work on a project that I had no interest in. Although I was disappointed, I recognized that I was a new member of the leadership team and could show other staff members my capabilities by serving on a committee that did not interest me. Had I requested to be moved or had a bad attitude about my committee assignment, my colleagues would have viewed me in a less than favorable way since I was the newest member of the leadership team. If I ended up having a bad attitude about the committee I was assigned to, any future requests to change committees would most likely be denied. At the conclusion of that school year, I requested to be moved to committees that better suit my skill set and was granted permission to change.

When to Apologize and When Not to Apologize

Being a strong and effective leader includes admitting when you are wrong and taking accountability for mistakes that you make. I am a firm believer in people will not judge you for the mistakes you make but for how you respond to your missteps. For example, I was having an extremely stressful day and a staff member that was on my team came into my class while I was teaching to run an idea by me. I wasn't thrilled that I was being interrupted during teaching for a question that could have been answered over email, so I was a bit curt with my colleague. After class, I recognized my mistake and immediately went to their room and apologized for our previous conversation. My apology was accepted, and we moved on from that conversation. If I did not take accountability for my actions and apologize, it is entirely possible that my colleague would have lost respect for me and our relationship would be damaged. Although I made the mistake of being curt, my apology directly to them was valued more than my mistake. It is okay to be wrong, recognize your own mistakes, take accountability, and move forward. Effective school leaders can take accountability and own up to mistakes. Staff members will appreciate this and view you as a leader, not a dictator.

Being a strong and effective leader also includes knowing when to not apologize for things that are not your fault. In my first year in a leadership position, I found that I was apologizing to parents/guardians and staff members for things that I was not involved in. I felt that my "over-apologizing" detracted from my leadership, and I will gladly explain my reasoning. Due to a hallway incident among three students, I was late to a meeting team meeting by a few minutes. I apologized for my tardiness and started the meeting, even though I was helping another staff member with an incident in the hallway. Instead of just saying "Sorry I was late" with no explanation, I should have structured my wording differently. I should have said, "Thank you for your patience with the meeting starting late today, I was helping with a hallway incident that required my immediate attention". Notice that I phrased this in a specific way that strikes an apologetic tone but explains the circumstances of my tardiness to staff members. I strongly believe how you phrase things as a leader is important to how others perceive and interact with you in your capacity as a school leader. I recommend not apologizing for things that you are not at fault for and structuring your sentences in a concise, yet meaningful way when interacting with the community and other staff members.

Seeking Constructive Feedback From Others

A way to better integrate into a new school and/or role is to seek constructive feedback from staff members that you supervise or work with on the leadership team. Seeking feedback on meetings you run or the professional development you lead will help you grow as a leader and allow you to meet the needs of your staff members. I wouldn't recommend verbally asking for feedback at the end of a meeting or professional development session because people may not feel comfortable sharing feedback out loud. When I seek feedback, I ensure that I do so by sending an email with a form attached. Below is an example of a feedback form you can send out to staff members to gather data on how things are going. I always ensure that staff members can submit the form anonymously so that I can get more responses. Anytime you send out a form where people have to put their name on it, many folks will not fill out the form for fear that it will be used against them in the future. I always ensure to include a spot for a staff member to tell me an area that is a "Pro" or an area they liked about my meeting or session. I then include an "Area of Growth" for staff members to give me any feedback. I always explain the form in the initial email I send to staff members so that they are not confused. You may be wondering; how does this relate to integrating into a school? As a new staff member and leader in the building, it is important to seek constructive feedback from staff members on how to better meet their needs. Not only will this increase your leadership in the school but show staff members that you are willing to listen to them and take what they say into consideration when you are planning meetings or professional development sessions. I believe garnering feedback will only further your integration into the leadership team and school.

Example Feedback Form

Staff Member Name (Optional):
Training/Meeting Date:
One "Pro" from the session:
One "Area of Growth" from the session:

Gauging the Social Climate

Being the "new person" at any school or workplace for that matter can be difficult since you may not be familiar with anyone at the school. Upon joining a new school in my first leadership position, I was lucky that I was surrounded by dozens of warm and friendly colleagues, that made me feel welcome. However, I am fully aware that my situation was ideal and not everyone is going to be as lucky as I was. Even though most colleagues were warm, not everyone was as friendly and open with me at first and that is okay since I was new and in a leadership position. Some teachers view school leaders as the "them" and the teachers as the "us". Essentially, what I am saying is that some teachers that are not in leadership positions have the "us versus them" mentality. The "us" meaning teachers and the "them" meaning any staff member in a leadership position. This mindset can occur for a variety of reasons due to personal experiences or people being jaded in general. Due to all these factors, some staff members may not feel comfortable being themselves around you for a while. Recognizing this possibility will help ease your transition into a new school and potentially temper any expectations you may have about all your new colleagues greeting you with warm welcomes. It will take time to build trust and build your creditability among staff members at your new school.

You Can't Please Everyone!

As a new leader, it is important to recognize that your actions and decisions will not please everyone that you work with – and that is okay! Being a leader involves making decisions for the best interest of the students, staff, and community at large. Not everyone is going to agree with your decisions, and you must be okay with that. It could be as simple as asking team members to not grade papers during meetings or as serious as asking a staff member to stop leaving fifteen minutes early each day since their planning period falls on the last period of the day. An example of when I made an unpopular decision is when I decided on something as simple as water. As a newly hired leader, I was told that I was in charge of collecting money each month to pay for the team's water delivery service for the team room. I did not want to "rock the boat" so I accepted this and figured I would try being in charge of it. What I found out was that about ten people would use the water in the team room but only five people paid consistently. When I sent out emails asking for payment, people would always "forget". So, I had a few choices I could make – either I unilaterally cancel the water service, I start fronting the money for the water, or I ask someone else to be in charge of the water delivery service that actually uses it (since I did not). I made the decision to email the entire team roughly two months into my position about the lack of consistent payments each month and I offered for someone else to take over with money collection since I was not using the water. I made it clear that I would be happy to help with the transition and gave a deadline on when I needed to hear back from team members. After a week, nobody emailed me asking to take over being in charge of the water delivery service, so I canceled it. Sure enough, at the next team meeting, I had three very unhappy team members who told me there were upset. In my conversation with them, I mentioned that they did not reply to my email and that I could not continue a water delivery service where only half of the people paid on time. I know this decision did not please everyone, but did I really want this to take up

30–40 minutes of my time each month? I know I could use that time more effectively to do my job as an instructional leader. Again, you can't please everyone!

The Past Sometimes is in the Present

Coming into a new school, you must be aware that some colleagues have positive and negative histories with each other. In the past, it is possible that some colleagues used to date or had a very bad falling out. Unless a trusted staff member gives you the history of this, there is no way that you will know. The reason I mention this is that some staff members may struggle to interact with each other because of things that happened in the past. Eventually, you will pick up on these things and use this knowledge to effectively lead. For example, Mr. Doe and Mrs. Poe used to date when they were in their twenties. Now they are in their forties and have their own lives, but still do not like each other. Having this knowledge, I would not recommend placing Mr. Doe and Mrs. Poe together in the same group during a professional development session. Obviously, there are going to be instances that they would have to interact together, but if you could avoid grouping them together, then do it!

Limit Social Media With Colleagues and Integrate at Your Own Pace

I would highly recommend limiting your social media access to new colleagues until you are fully comfortable with the specific person that adds you. If a person at work adds you on social media, I would leave the request pending until you can trust them. Part of integrating into a new school or leadership team involves developing friendships or "work friendships" with others. This does not mean you are obligated to share your social media pages with anyone. I made the mistake of letting co-workers add me in the past before I got to know them. This led to folks asking me questions about my personal life that I would not necessarily enjoy speaking about at work. For example, I went on a vacation with my girlfriend and posted a picture of the trip. I took a personal day off, which is perfectly okay. The next Monday, I had a colleague make a comment to me about missing work to "have fun" skiing. The funny thing is, I was not skiing and was just on vacation. The person saw my picture and assumed I was skiing and took it upon themselves to tell other people I was skiing. After my conversation with her, four other people made comments to me asking about skiing. I learned a social media lesson the hard way! I should never have accepted friend requests from colleagues I did not know that well. Another option you can consider is to add colleagues but severely limit their access to your profiles. This is the option that I have used for the past few years to avoid any more rumors being spread about what I do in my free time.

The Microscope Will Be on You, Make Sure You Shine!

As a new leader in the building, the microscope will be on you and that is okay! Being an instructional leader means that you will contribute to setting the tone of the leadership team. I am not saying this to put extra pressure on you, I just want to help new leaders become aware that their actions are being looked at by everyone. For example, a new leader got hired at my school and wore jeans on a Friday. After they wore the jeans, they told me and five staff members, then asked him if it is okay to wear jeans on Friday. Being new to the school, he had no idea that jeans were against the dress code. Sure enough, on the following Friday there were a few staff members that wore jeans because a school leader wore them the previous week. Something as simple as wearing jeans can be homed in on and seen by school staff. When I first started my leadership position, I noticed people would notice the time I arrived to work, the time I left work, and what I wore. Simple comments such as, "You don't have to wear a tie", "I see you got here early today, working hard?", or "Why do you get here so early every day?" Even though all of these comments are in theory harmless, they showed me that being a new leader in a school will increase the spotlight on me. On top of this, I was the youngest member of the leadership team and the second youngest staff member in the building, so I recognized that a lot of folks were watching me closely because of the age gap between myself and other staff members. Again, the point I am trying to make is that being a new leader will include having a microscope being pointed at you. Through your winning system, having a microscope being pointed at you will not faze you at all!

Final Thoughts

Effectively integrating into a new school and leadership team will take time but will be rewarding. Each school and leadership team will have unique dynamics and structures that will take getting used to regardless of your prior experience. By maintaining a winning system, you will be able to better adapt to the challenges you will encounter during your first year regardless of the circumstances of what you encounter. Whether it is serving on a committee that you do not necessarily enjoy, making a mistake with a colleague during a meeting, maintaining email etiquette, or something as simple as wearing jeans, there are going to be trials and tribulations of being a new leader in a building. Recognizing that there will be some challenges throughout your first year will help you face those challenges head-on and be more prepared for all of the things you will face. By taking accountability for your actions, being adaptable, being consistent, and maintaining your organization, you are going to excel throughout your first year of leading.

3

Creating Meaningful Professional Development

Developing meaningful and engaging professional development for staff members is not an easy task. In many ways, my approach to creating trainings and professional development is similar to my mindset of creating lessons for students. I must take into consideration the strengths and weaknesses of the group I am presenting to and differentiate the session to meet their needs. I will describe how to differentiate professional development more in depth later in this chapter. The point I am trying to make is that creating meaningful professional development is part of your role as a school leader. Education is a world of constantly revolving buzzwords and new ideas which ultimately help move the profession forward. While staying up to date with the latest and greatest buzzwords is important, it will not define your training session or professional development session as successful. How you deliver training is important, but **why** you are delivering a specific training is more important.

Start With Solving a Problem or Issue

Before I begin to plan any professional development session or training that I am going to deliver to staff members, I like to start with identifying the problem or issue I plan on addressing. I feel that identifying a specific topic help guide the session and the structure of what I am going to implement. The problem or issue can be a variety of different topics or issues that can arise in a school. For example, a school district just implemented a new online system

DOI: 10.4324/9781003230274-4

for teachers to use for grading, assignment distribution, and parent communication. If I were to start planning a professional development session to address, I would consider sending a survey out to staff members asking them to identify three areas they need help with using the new system. After reading the results of the survey, I would be able to identify common problems that staff members I supervise were having. After identifying the problem or issues, I would be able to begin planning a meaningful training to address the needs of staff members. Surveying staff members before developing a training will enhance and amplify your staff's voice and chances to give input on the trainings they receive. This not only increases your credibility with staff members but shows that you are willing to take feedback from staff members that you supervise. Another example of "starting with a problem" would be if you received multiple emails about the new attendance policy. If many staff members are confused on how to implement the new attendance policy, you could develop a training session to address this issue. Carefully going over the new policy and answering common questions will ideally increase the effectiveness of the new policy and allow staff members to implement it with more fidelity. Developing professional development sessions through the lens of problem solving has allowed me to make more meaningful professional development for staff members over the years and give staff members a voice in what trainings they receive.

Differentiation Is Key

Differentiating your professional development sessions is key to engaging staff members in a meaningful way. We all know what differentiation looks like in the classroom, but it may be hard for new leaders to envision what differentiation looks like in a professional development session. The fact of the matter is differentiation in a professional development session can look like a variety of different things. Differentiation can mean grouping staff members based on the subject they teach, skill level on a particular topic, or grade level they teach. Differentiation during a training session can also be grouping participants by their skill level on a particular skill or topic. I do want to note, I highly recommend not grouping staff members by skill level before the meeting begins. This can lead to staff members being offended by your perception of their skill level on a particular topic. I always recommend that staff members self-identify whether they are a beginner, intermediate, or advanced for a specific training. For example, if I was conducting a training with two other leaders on best practices for online assessments, I would state, "Okay, now we are going to do small groups based on skill level. If you identify as a beginner, you are with me, if you identify as an intermediate go with Mr. Doe, if you identify as advanced go with Mrs. Poe". This allows staff members to think honestly about their own skill level on a particular topic. If a staff member feels either too advanced or that their group is too advanced once it begins, they can make the decision to move groups themselves. If nobody identifies as a particular skill level, a second trainer can be added to a different group. For example, if nobody identified as an intermediate skill level for online assessments, Mr. Doe can join the beginner or advanced group. Minor modifications like this are totally okay! Again, allowing staff members the ability to choose their own skill level will avoid any resentment toward you.

Making Trainings Relevant

In relation to differentiating professional development sessions, it is also important to consider the experience of the staff members you are delivering the training to. Being a new teacher does not mean less competence as much as being a veteran teacher does not mean competence in teaching. Some staff members may come in with an attitude of "We did this last year. Why do we have to do it again," so it is important to consult with other leaders or staff members about past trainings. However, even if a similar training was implemented in the past, think how you can make the current training relevant to this school year. For example, if a training was implemented the previous school year on using state testing data, you can easily develop a training or professional development session that focuses on that current school year. Even if a teacher "looped" with their students to the next grade level, test data always changes and will impact the instructional decisions of teachers. To be more specific, I will give an example. "Mr. Katzel is a new leader at John Doe Middle School and wants to develop a training for the sixth grade team. The training will focus on testing data for English Language Arts. But a wrench was thrown in Mr. Katzel's plans! A teacher on his team told him they did a very similar training the previous year, and each teacher knows how to access the testing data. Mr. Katzel's original plans will not work, so he must pivot. To differentiate the training from the previous years, Mr. Katzel made modifications so that the training no longer focused on accessing the data. Mr. Katzel will briefly go over how to access student test scores, but now focus on how to interpret the test scores and go over two examples of how teachers can use the data to differentiate class readings. Mr. Katzel was successfully able to pivot his training to make it relevant. Even though parts of the training were covered the previous year, he made it relevant to his team". No staff member wants to sit through a training they have done in the past or that they feel has no relevance to their current work. Pivoting in planning and developing trainings or professional development sessions are key to winning your first year in leadership. In fact, this directly aligns with the "adaptability" pillar of my winning system. To further prepare you for your leadership role, I want to mention that there will be times that trainings or professional developments do not go as planned, and that is okay! During the session, there may be common misconceptions or questions that many staff members have, and you will end up addressing immediately in the training. For example, one time I was doing a training on transferring materials from the cloud into an online classroom during the Covid-19 pandemic. I did not foresee that many teachers were using the incorrect internet browser, which was inhibiting their ability to transfer over content. In the middle of my training, I had to adapt and pivot the session into showing staff members how to download the proper web browser to link up to the cloud. This took up more time than I would have hoped, but if I did not address this immediately, my professional development session would not have gone as planned. Being adaptable allowed me to address the needs of the educators I was working with.

Building the Capacity of Your Team

Later in this chapter, I am going to show an example of a training you can implement with a small or large group. But before I get into the specifics of a particular training, I want to discuss how you can build the capacity of other staff members through collaboration. Regardless of where you work, there are bound to be a few individuals who are jaded towards your school or the profession of teaching in general. Maybe the teachers are jaded due to not being hired for leadership experiences in the past. It is possible they feel that they are wearing the "golden handcuffs" and cannot leave teaching, or they could have even applied for the position you have and interviewed against you. Whatever the reason may be, working with jaded teachers or employees can be a tricky process and difficult to navigate. A way to increase your positive interactions with the jaded teacher would be to involve them in planning a training in which they excel. For example, Mr. John Doe has been working at Stephen Katzel Middle School for the past twenty years. He has applied to numerous leadership positions and never was hired for them. He feels frustrated that younger and less experienced teachers are in the leadership positions he desires. Mr. Doe also feels that seniority should be taken into consideration when hiring, and that he has put in his time at the school. A new eighth grade team leader was hired, and Mr. Doe has not been engaging in the team meetings. However, the new team leader notices that Mr. Doe is very good at developing and implementing classroom discussions for his English classes. The new team leader then asks Mr. Doe to help plan a training on classroom discussions for eighth grade. By enlisting the help of Mr. Doe, his voice and opinions feel recognized and that they matter. In my experience, Mr. Doe would then feel more valued and ideally less jaded in his interactions with the new team leader. Enlisting Mr. Doe to help with the training also builds his capacity to lead in the future if he is still interested in leadership positions. Something as simple as asking staff members to co-lead a training session will foster collaboration and ideally decrease the extent of negative or jaded feelings towards working in a school. Other ways to engage and increase participation from jaded staff members are to show recognition of their work or ask them to lead a small committee. I am not saying to give preferential treatment to staff members who are jaded. However, improving their morale will certainly help improve the school's moral.

Creating an Engaging Professional Development Session

Creating an engaging professional development session/training for staff members may seem like a daunting task for new leaders. However, following a similar format as to how you plan lessons for students is important. Also, asking yourself the right questions while planning a training is important as well. What take away is my staff going to get from this training? How can staff members implement this training into their classrooms? Am I talking during the entire training or am I giving staff the chance to collaborate? Asking these questions will ideally guide your planning to offer meaningful professional development for staff members. Each school-based leader has their own style, and you will have to figure out how you conduct professional development with your staff. The commonality in each successful professional development session I have been a part of is that the session was engaging and did not involve having a person speak at the group the entire session. Another factor of successful trainings has been that they were relevant to the work in my classroom and that I was able to take away new knowledge from the session. Keeping all this mind, I am going to delve into a training that can be done with a small or large group.

Each school year, I like to conduct a professional development session that focuses on school-wide data with specific data points related to the team I am working with. Before technology became advanced, it was difficult to analyze data in large quantities. However, with technology being so advanced, accessing student data is easier than ever. Conducting a professional development session related to school-wide data will help your team, department, or whole staff become more aware of student populations in the school and be better prepared to meet the needs of all students. For example, it is entirely possible that your school district re-drew the boundary lines to determine which elementary schools feed into the local middle schools. This can change the socio-economic backgrounds of your students and present different challenges than you encountered in previous years. Constantly looking at data is an important aspect of being a leader, regardless of if you are a team leader or department chair. Below are three ways that you can construct a professional development session relating to your school's data points. I would recommend conducting this training during pre-service week to inform staff members of the student populations in the school for that particular year. I also advocate for new leaders to conduct this training with their staff to start the year with a training that is relevant to their students and ultimately their lesson plans. I will delve into the structure of this training and how you can make it engaging for a group of ten or a group of eighty staff members. I always intend to develop trainings that can be used for a variety of groups, regardless of the number of participants or subject matters that they teach.

Start With a Hook

We have all participated in training sessions that were not engaging for a variety of reasons. It is possible that the presenter spoke the entire time, the material was not relevant, or that the session was not engaging. How a facilitator begins a session is key to setting the tone and purpose of the session for all participants, and it can make or break the effectiveness of what is being presented. Keeping this in mind, I always suggest new leaders plan professional development sessions with a "hook" that engages the staff member in the content or data that is going to be delivered. When starting a professional development session that involves data, I always give the chance for staff to make predictions on specific metrics. The purpose of this is not to fill the first five minutes of a training with an activity, it is to allow staff members to be actively engaged with the training. Figure 3.1 exemplifies how to frame a professional development on data and can be handed out to staff members as they enter the room. I always ensure to include a title on any handout I give to staff members to make sure it is clear to them what the session was about. Also, I could have easily given the participants of the training all the data as they walked in but allowing time for predictions allows me to easily transition to a second part of the training. The next step of the training involves having staff members discuss their predictions with a partner or a small group. I want to briefly discuss why it is important for staff members to be able to choose their own groups or partner to speak with. I have worked with people that strongly advocate pre-determining groups before training sessions, but I highly recommend against this. When you preset which teachers are paired together, it can be somewhat patronizing if there is not a purpose to choosing groups for the session. For example, it may make sense to group staff members by content area if a training is being conducted analyzing each department's student achievement data. Other than very targeted reasons, I always let staff members choose their groups and I believe this adds to the effectiveness of trainings that I have delivered. After allowing staff members to discuss their predictions, I delve right into the data.

Sixth Grade Data Analysis PD

Part #1- Predictions

    1. What percentage of our student population is…..

Male-
Female-

2. What percentage of our student population is…..

ESOL (English as a Second Language)-
FARMS (Free & Reduced Lunch) -
Receive Special Education Services (IEP or 504 Plan)-

3. What percentage of our student population is…..

African American-
American Indian-
Asian-
Caucasian-
Hawaiian/Pacific Islander-
Hispanic-
Multiracial-

4. What percentage of our 6th graders are absent in the last 10 days? (Please average the numbers).

Figure 3.1 Data Sheet for a Training

Discussing and Formatting Data

When I present data to staff members during a professional development session, I do my best to keep all the information on one page. In the past, I gave staff members five pages of data, which resulted in some people being overwhelmed and disengaged due to the amount of data I gave out. The old saying "less is more" is something that I follow and implement into my leadership philosophy. Figure 3.2 exemplifies this philosophy and shows a lot of data points, but all on one page. This allows staff members to not feel overwhelmed by the amount of data that they are looking at. Presenting data on the number of students with limited English proficiency, number of students receiving free and reduced lunches, and the number of students receiving special education services enables staff members to further understand the background of the students that they teach. I always include data metrics comparing the school that I am at to the "average" school in the district to allow staff members to see how our student population is similar to or different than the average school. When I present the data shown in Figure 3.2, I allow staff members to take a few minutes to analyze the numbers. Then, I allow staff members to discuss the data in small groups to encourage collaboration

DATA CRUNCH		
Out of 1,000 students . . .	Out of 1,000 students . . .	Out of 1,000 students . . .
51 students have limited English language proficiency at our school.	We have 100 FARMS students at our school.	We have 70 students receiving special education services at our school.
A school with a similar number of students in our district would have an average of 187 students with limited English proficiency,	A school with a similar number of students in our district has an average 401 students classified as FARMS,	A school with a similar number of students in our district would have on average of 150 students receiving special education services,
Or . . . roughly 4 times the number of LEP students at our school.	Or . . . roughly 4 times the number of FARMS students at our school.	Or . . . roughly double the number of students receiving special education services at our school.

Figure 3.2 Data Sheet for a Training

among the participants. After a few minutes of discussion, I always ask that groups fill out the data chart and answer two reflection questions as a group. You will be able to make determinations on how long you want groups to speak before having them share their thoughts and ideas. I always ask that groups share their reflections on the data because everyone approaches data differently. Allowing other groups to share their ideas may help other teachers and leaders in the room discover a metric or look at data in a different way. Having groups of staff members share also makes the session more engaging because staff members have the chance to talk. Again, when sitting through trainings where the instructor is the only one speaking, the lack of engagement from staff is typically high. Figure 3.3 shows you how you can ask two

---

Sixth Grade Data Analysis PD

Part #2 – Data Analysis

1. What percentage of our student population is . . .

   Male – 49.1%
   Female – 50.9%

2. What percentage of our student population is . . .

   ESOL (English as a Second Language) – 5.1%
   FARMS (Free & Reduced Lunch) – 10.1%
   Receiving Special Education Services (IEP or 504 Plan) – 7%

3. What percentage of our student population is . . .

   African American – 12%
   American Indian – 1%
   Asian – 15%
   Caucasian – 20%
   Hawaiian/Pacific Islander – 4%
   Hispanic – 46%
   Multiracial– 2%

4. What percentage of our sixth graders have been absent in the last 10 days? (Please average the numbers).

   5.7%

5. What data points surprised your group?

6. What school initiatives can be developed to increase attendance in sixth grade?

Figure 3.3 Data Sheet for a Training

"closing" questions to end the session. I always end each professional development thanking staff members for their time and reminding them that I will send a brief survey asking them for feedback.

Garnering Feedback From Staff Members

After conducting professional development sessions, I believe it is important to ask for feedback from staff members to address any lingering questions and to improve your future professional development sessions. I typically send an email the next business day to any staff member that was involved in the training. Below is an example of an email and short survey you can send out to get feedback. Most school districts pay for services that allow you to make surveys or have cloud services that allow you to create surveys as well. When you send out the survey, make sure that you make it optional for staff members to put their names. If you make it mandatory that staff members put their name on the survey, then you will get less honest feedback since staff members won't want any retaliation for voicing their honest opinions. To further expand on this, some criticism will be unfair, so take the feedback with a grain of salt if you get a crazy response. I also want to mention to always remember to be adaptable when conducting professional development sessions. Some sessions will not go as planned for a variety of reasons. There can be questions you did not anticipate, or a certain activity may run longer than expected. Being adaptable as a facilitator is part of being a good leader and presenter. Staff members will appreciate your flexibility in allowing discussions to progress and will ultimately appreciate your adaptability in general.

Example Email

Good Morning,

I wanted to thank all staff members for actively participating and engaging in the "Data Chat" professional development session. Attached in the email is the presentation and handout from the session. Below is a link to a survey about the professional development session. **All survey responses are confidential,** and you do not need to put your name on your response. Please let me know if you have any questions.

Thank You,

Stephen

Example Survey

Name (Optional) –
Did you find the training relevant? Please explain in 1–2 sentences.
Were the training materials useful? Please explain in 1–2 sentences.
How do you think the training could be improved? Please explain in 1–2 sentences.

Allowing staff members to give you feedback on professional development sessions will increase your leadership in your school. You are garnering staff feedback to evaluate your session which shows that you are a reflective leader. In many schools, staff members feel that their voices are not heard by the leadership team and there can be an "us" versus "them" mentality. Asking for feedback from staff members helps build bridges among staff and the leadership team. Being viewed as a reflective leader who is open to feedback will increase the trust staff members have in you as a leader. Garnering feedback from staff members will make you a better leader and facilitator for future professional development sessions.

When Professional Development Is Scheduled for After School

There will inevitably be times when a professional development session will have to be scheduled after school. It can take the form of a staff meeting or training session, but direct initiatives pop up that require holding meetings after school. Sometimes there can be staff members who have after school commitments like childcare issues or family commitments that make it difficult to attend after-school meetings. If this is the case, try to problem-solve with the staff member and collaboratively come up with solutions. Try to give staff members as much notice as possible when a meeting is going to be held after school.

Co-Planning Professional Development With Staff Members

When working an instructional leader, you will encounter extremely strong teachers who are innovative and inspiring. As a new leader in the building, I would work on identifying strong teachers to help co-plan professional development throughout the year. For example, if I conducted a classroom observation of Mrs. Doe, I may notice that she is an expert on developing teaching stations for her class. Since I believe that other staff members would benefit from knowing how to conduct stations in this manner, I would ask Mrs. Doe to co-plan a professional development session. If Mrs. Doe did not want to present to the staff but gave me permission to show the classroom materials she created, I would make it a point to mention that the training I developed was inspired by a lesson I saw Mrs. Doe develop. Whenever possible, engaging with staff members to co-plan trainings will build the capacity of staff members and show that you are a collaborative leader.

Do Not Meet for the Sake of Meeting

As a leader it is important to not schedule meetings for the sake of meetings. Not everything can be done through emails, but in particular instances a meeting can be replaced with a short email. If I realized that everything was covered in the previous two meetings in a week, I may do a "virtual" meeting. To be more specific, if a meeting would have only been five minutes, I would tell the staff members over an email what I was going to cover in the meeting. Whenever I cancel a meeting, I always offer any staff members to come to my room or office to discuss any questions that they have. You can also make a short recoding of yourself and upload the recording to a video site, which then allows you to send the link to staff members. I have done this in the past when meetings would be too short to justify calling, but I still had some information to give to staff. Giving staff members more time to lesson plan or grade will be appreciated and they will view you as a more effective leader because you do not call meetings just for the sake of meeting.

Final Thoughts

Creating meaningful professional development opportunities for staff is a key aspect of winning your first year of leadership. Whether you were hired as a team leader, staff development teacher, master teacher, department chair, or administrator, being able to develop and effectively deliver professional development is a key part of your job as a leader. Using relevant data in professional development sessions will add creditability to your leadership in the eyes of your staff and allow your professional development to be relevant to the staff you supervise. Being attentive to how you structure the groups in your trainings and how you structure the session will contribute overwhelmingly to the successes and failures of the trainings that you develop. Making sure that you start each training with a "hook" will further the engagement of participants in your training and allow you to introduce the topic with ease. Allowing staff members chances to discuss the topic of your training will offer further engagement but also fosters a positive school environment.

4

Facilitating Parent Conferences and Mentoring Programs

Regardless of your position as a school-based leader, you will be part of parent-teacher conferences in some capacity. In fact, as a school leader, chances are that you will be one of the people that have to plan parent-teacher conferences. There are numerous ways you can plan for a successful parent-teacher conference and it will vary based on the structure your school chooses. In this chapter, I will delve into a few different ways you can structure your conferences and the pros and cons of each method. School leaders set the tone for parent-teacher conferences and ultimately are responsible for setting up staff members for success. I have been part of many different parent-teacher conference formats as a teacher and a leader. Being on both sides has given me insight into what works and what does not work. Regardless of your current position, it is also important to know the importance of mentoring programs and how to structure them. It doesn't matter how successful your school is, there will always be an achievement gap no matter where you work. I define the achievement gap as measurable gaps in academic achievement in specific groups of students. Depending on your school, different groups can be part of the achievement gap. Developing and implementing a mentoring program will ideally help close the achievement gap at your school. In this chapter, I will discuss a few different ways you can structure a mentoring program and how to determine goals for the program, measure goals for the program, and train staff members to help implement a successful mentoring program. Without staff buy-in, no mentoring program will be successful.

DOI: 10.4324/9781003230274-5

Running an Individual Parent-Teacher Conference

Before delving into parent-teacher conferences, I briefly want to talk about individual parent-teacher meetings that occur throughout the year in case you have never run a meeting before. Sometimes, parents or guardians request to meet with one teacher or all of their student's teachers. Knowing how to start and end the meeting is important. I always recommend starting meetings with introductions of whomever is attending the meeting. After introductions, I recommend stating the purpose of the meeting and when staff members present at the meeting need to leave. Setting this time expectation will ideally control the pace of the meeting. After stating the purpose of the meeting, I would have staff members share their data or insights, then I would allow for the parent/guardian to respond or ask questions. Throughout the meeting, I would take notes and write down "next steps". At the end of the meeting, I would thank the parent or guardian for their time and tell them how I plan to follow up. During the meeting, it is important to be additive, and not repetitive. Also, if you envision that the meeting is going to be difficult, you can have a pre-conference with staff members beforehand to go over talking points. I know that this is a super broad overview of running an individual meeting and this was intentional. Depending on the needs of your school and the specific meeting, different meetings will be run different ways. My goal was to at least give you a blueprint on how to run an individual meeting in case you have never done so before.

Starting the Parent-Teacher Conference Process

Each school that I have worked at has conducted parent-teacher conferences in different ways to best meet the needs of the students, parents, guardians, and the community. There is not one correct way to plan and implement a successful parent-teacher conference. However, as a leader, it is your job to help determine how to structure the conferences, who to invite to the conferences, how many conferences to have, and how involved teachers are in the planning of the conferences. The first step I recommend in planning for successful parent-teacher conferences is to assess the degree of student achievement. I have worked at schools that have at least 50% of the students with at least one D or E and I have worked at schools where over 50% of the student population is on the honor roll. Needless to say, parent-teacher conferences at both schools were run very differently to varying degrees of success. To determine what route you are going to take in planning for the event, the first thing you need to do is run a grade report to determine the grades of the grade level you are planning conferences for. It is important to run this report to see how many students received a D or E in specific courses and how many D's and E's each student received. I want to note that most school districts have the software to pull this type of report. If you are unsure how to pull this report, please ask a colleague and they will be able to show you. Unintentionally, this gives you data on how teachers are distributing grades, but that will be discussed in a future chapter. After running the report, you will be able to determine how to best run your parent-teacher conferences. I am going to discuss different methods in approaching the event through the use of data. Making data-driven decisions will help guide you throughout the leadership process and allow you to validate specific decisions that you make over time. Whenever I plan grade-level or school-wide events, I ensure I have some piece of data to reinforce the major decisions I make throughout the planning process. I am going to delve into a hypothetical planning process for a grade level with 300 students.

Scenario 1 – Invite Everyone

Sixth Grade Achievement Data – Stephen Katzel Middle School

Number of students	Number of students with a D or E in one course	Number of students with a D or E in two courses	Number of students with a D or E in three courses	Number of students with a D or E in four or more courses
300	123	17	9	12

For Scenario #1, we are going to look at an example middle school that as a student population of 300 sixth grade students. You are a newly hired leader and are asked to plan conferences using this data in mind. In total, roughly 50% of all students at the school have at least one D or E in their classes for the quarter. After looking at this data, it is obvious that students are falling behind with their classes, and engaging the community to ensure a high turnout is extremely important to closing the achievement gap at your school. With this many students having non-passing D's or E's, it is imperative that you invite each parent and guardian to the parent-teacher conferences. I want to note, this format only works if your school gives you enough time to have conferences and that the conferences start early in the day, and finish at night. If you are able to, I would schedule parent-teacher conferences on a half day, so that you can start them at 12 pm and finish them at 7 pm. It is important to give teachers and staff members an hour off for dinner from 5 pm to 6 pm, so that they can have a break and be fresh to finish out conferences. I always like to offer conference times in the evening to allow parents the chance to attend conferences even if they are not able to get off work by 5 pm. Even if I send out a notification weeks or months in advance about conferences, the reality is that not all families can attend because of work. When planning a parent conference day that lasts this long, I always ensure to make this **the only day** of parent-teacher conferences so that my staff does not get burned-out. If you can, I would send out the date and time of the conference as soon as possible to the entire community through an email and a letter that is sent home. Remember, for this format, every student's parent or guardian is invited to the conference with teachers. Later on, I will discuss how to make that possible, it is doable! Below is an example of a letter or email you can send to the entire grade level to invite them to parent-teacher conferences. I also make it a point to include "guardians" in all of my communication to the community because we cannot assume any student's background and who is taking care of them.

Example Letter to the Community

Dear Parents & Guardians,

My name is Stephen Katzel, and I am excited to be your sixth-grade team leader for the 20XX-20XX school year. The first quarter is ending on November 15th and we are excited to announce parent-teacher conferences on November 23rd from 12 pm to 7 pm at John Doe Middle School. However, please note that from 5 pm to 6 pm, teachers will be eating dinner and not be able to take any conferences. Parent conferences will be through a "walk-in" format for the entirety of the conferences. Each sixth-grade teacher will be available to conference and will be set up in the gymnasium with a table, computer, and timer. Each conference with the teacher will last no more than 10 minutes due to the high number of parents and guardians attending the conference. If you need more time with a specific teacher, please schedule a phone call for a different time. While teachers are conferencing with other groups, please wait at least ten feet away from the teacher's table to give other families privacy in their conversations. The grade level administrator and I will be walking around the gymnasium for the entirety of the conferences to assist you. Please email me or call the school to ask any questions.

Thank You,

Mr. Stephen Katzel

In the letter, I was descriptive as to how the event would be structured, when the event would take place, and how staff members would be made available throughout the day. In total, teachers may be able to see up to 36 students if each 10-minute slot was filled. In my experience, most teachers have between 120–150 students, so being able to meet with 42 parents and guardians would cover a high percentage of the students they teach. Setting up each teacher in the gymnasium, cafeteria, or media center is a key aspect of planning this format successfully. If you are going to invite hundreds of people from the community to come to the school, having everyone in one place solves many logistical problems. Having teachers stay in their room for conferences creates logistical nightmares and mass confusion on conference day. If you let teachers stay in their rooms for conferences, be prepared to have to answer hundreds of questions (yes, hundreds) from parents and guardians asking what room number specific teachers are located in. Even if a teacher does an amazing job communicating the room that they are located in, it is super hard finding up to seven different rooms if you are unfamiliar with the school. In all major entrances to the buildings, make signs that point folks in the direction of the conferences to minimize any potential confusion among the community. In the letter, I also make it very clear that teachers are unable to conference for an hour to allow for them to eat dinner. It would be very unwise to not allow teachers a break for dinner and I highly suggest ordering the staff dinner for that night. Something as small as a pizza dinner goes a long way in how people view you as a leader. Nobody will be thinking "Ugh! Mr. Katzel doesn't care about us; he asks us to stay late and can't even provide staff with a snack".

Allowing parents and guardians to attend conferences through a "walk-in" format will reduce the amount of planning you will have to do for the conferences. You will not have to develop protocols to invite community members and you will not have to make a criterion to determine which students are invited. At this particular school, half of the students have at least one non-passing grade. Having a walk-in format will increase the number of parents/guardians that attend the conferences and ideally lead to a high percentage of the community attending conferences. I also make it a point to ask community members to give teachers in conferences with other families some space so there is privacy. I personally would feel uneasy discussing personal things about a student when a stranger is close by. About three days before the parent-teacher conference date, I would re-send the original letter out to the community through email and by giving each student a paper copy. Some families may not be able to easily access the internet or have a phone with data, so giving students a handout to take home furthers your ability to be a responsive leader to all students, regardless of their background. I also want to mention that it is imperative you go over the structure of the parent-teacher conferences during a team meeting. I would show teachers the letter before I send it out, along with the data that I pulled on the number of students that received a D or E in a course for that specific quarter. Showing teachers that you are making data-driven decisions will further validate your decision-making in terms of how to structure parent-teacher conferences. There may be a few teachers who are not thrilled with having to conference with anyone who walks in. However, at the end of the day, school leaders have a responsibility to promote student achievement and in turn support the community. Going over the plan and answering questions from teachers will ideally ease their concerns and get the team on the same page before telling the community the details of the event.

I want to reiterate that there isn't a correct or incorrect way to plan and implement parent-teacher conferences. This method is extremely powerful for schools that have a lot of students that need extra support. Engaging with the entire community can seem like a daunting task due to the amount of people you are inviting into your building. However, centralizing the location of every teacher will streamline the logistical nightmare of having teachers conduct conferences in their classrooms. This method of conducting parent-teacher conferences will allow you to connect parents and guardians with teachers that may have never been in touch with before. Ask other leaders in your building to help you walk around the conference location to assist parents and guardians throughout the night. Having school leaders in one location will allow the night to run smoother and give teachers another layer of support if they have to deal with a hostile parent or guardian or if they need help during a meeting. It is a lot easier to flag down a school leader in a centralized location than it is to call someone on a cell phone in a classroom. Next, I will go over how to conduct parent conferences in a different format to meet the needs of students based on data analysis.

Scenario 2 – "Invite-Only" Conferences

Sixth Grade Achievement Data – Stephen Katzel Middle School

Number of students	Number of students with a D or E in one course	Number of students with a D or E in two courses	Number of students with a D or E in three courses	Number of students with a D or E in four or more courses
300	14	2	6	3

For Scenario #2, we are going to look at an example middle school that has a student population of 300 sixth grade students. You are a newly hired leader and asked to plan conferences using this data in mind. In total, roughly 8.3% of all students at the school have at least one D or E in their classes for the quarter. After looking at this data, it is obvious that some students are falling behind with their classes, but the majority of the student population is performing well in their classes. As a new leader, you are faced with a "good" predicament. Since over 90% of your student population did not have a failing grade, it wouldn't make sense to invite each parent and guardian to conference with teachers. What makes the most sense would be to **only** invite the parents and guardians of students with at least one D or E to conference with teachers. Now, if a parent or guardian wants to meet with a teacher, you cannot deny them that chance. Shortly, I will explain how to structure this format where specific parents and guardians of students are identified to be invited while limiting how you open it up to the community at large. If you are able to, I would schedule parent-teacher conferences on a half day, so that you can start them at 12 pm and finish them at 7 pm. Just like the previous scenario, having a large time frame is important so that families that work and cannot get off can ultimately attend the parent-teacher conferences. Again, send out the conference date as soon as possible. Also, remember to go over the structure of the parent conferences during a team meeting so that you can answer any questions.

Example Letter to the Community

Dear Parents & Guardians,

My name is Stephen Katzel, and I am excited to be your sixth-grade team leader for the 20XX-20XX school year. The first quarter is ending on November 15th and we are excited to announce parent-teacher conferences on November 23rd from 12 pm to 7 pm at John Doe Middle School. However, please note that from 5 pm to 6 pm, teachers will be eating dinner and not be able to take any conferences.

Parent conferences will be "invitation only" for all parent-teacher conferences. If you are invited to a parent-teacher conference, you will receive an email from me explaining the process on November 14th. However, if you do not receive an invitation to conferences but want to meet with your student's teachers, please send me an email no later than November 18th. Please email me or call the school to ask any questions.

Thank You,

Mr. Stephen Katzel (6th Grade Team Leader)

If less than 10% of your student population has failing grades, I recommend making parent-teacher conferences invitation only. Making conferences "invitation only" allows teachers to spend more time with families that have students who are struggling in school than with families of students who are getting higher marks. Notice in my letter that I did not completely shut out parents and guardians of students that will not ultimately receive an invitation to conferences. If a parent or guardian wants to meet with a teacher, you cannot tell them no. However, by structuring conferences as "invite only", I am making sure that teachers are more accessible to families that may need to talk to three or more teachers about their student. It is not easy taking off work and coming to conferences, so accessibility is key to events involving the community. In my experience, when you make parent-teacher conferences "invite-only", you will only get a handful of parents and guardians that reach out requesting a conference. Something I do want to note, if there are students that aren't struggling academically but socially or emotionally, it would be acceptable and encouraged to invite their parents and guardians to the conferences. Success for our students is not solely defined by their academic performance and students that are not doing well socially and emotionally could benefit from having their caretaker meet with their teachers. Please use your professional discretion when making a decision on inviting students that are struggling emotionally or socially. You can ask a grade-level team leader or the counseling department for any students they feel would benefit from conferences for social and emotional reasons if you are unsure about who to invite. When I invite parents and guardians to conferences, I ensure I include more information than the initial letter that goes out to the community.

Example Invitation

Dear Parents & Guardians,

My name is Stephen Katzel, and I am excited to be your Sixth Grade team leader for the 20XX-20XX school year. The first quarter is ending on November 15th and we are excited to announce parent-teacher conferences on November 23rd from 12 pm to 7 pm at John Doe Middle School. However, please note that from 5 pm to 6 pm, teachers will be eating dinner and not be able to take any conferences. I am excited to invite you to parent-teacher conferences on November 15th. Each sixth-grade teacher available to conference and will be set up in the gymnasium with a table, computer, and timer. Each conference with the teacher will last no more than 20 minutes due to the high number of parent and guardians attending the conference. If you need more time with a specific teacher, please schedule a phone call for a different time. While teachers are conferencing with other groups, please wait at least ten feet away from the teacher's table to give other families privacy in their conversations. The other administrators and I will be walking around the gymnasium for the entirety of the conferences to assist you. Please email me or call the school to ask any questions.

Thank You,

Mr. Stephen Katzel (Sixth Grade Team Leader)

This method is extremely powerful for schools that do not have a lot of students that need extra support. When there are less conferences scheduled, teachers will be able to spend more time with parent and guardians that attend the conference. Notice that for this format, each conference was allocated 20 minutes instead of 10 minutes like the first format. When you have less people, you have more time to meet. This method of parent-teacher conferences allows you to connect parents and guardians with teachers for a meaningful amount of time without feeling rushed. Some leaders may feel inclined to make a sign up for parents to choose specific time slots for specific teachers if they use the "invitation-only" format for conferences. I would not recommend trying to schedule specific times because people run late, and people do not show up for conferences. It is a logistical nightmare trying to coordinate specific time slots for specific teachers and for specific parents and guardians. If you want to try this method of scheduling, you will have more chaos on the day of conferences than a leader who allows there to be a "walk in" format. I have seen conferences run late or a parent or guardian not show, which create major scheduling issues the day of conferences. For example, Mrs. Doe is running late and really wants to talk to Mr. Katzel about her son's grade. Mrs. Doe missed her 3:00 appointment though. She makes it to school at 5:30, but Mr. Katzel is booked up until his last conference of the day. Mrs. Doe is now waiting for Mr. Katzel to finish, but his other appointments showed up and now he has to leave at 7:00 to pick up his kids. Now Mrs. Doe is frustrated she cannot meet with him because she ran late and has a bad view of the school and Mr. Katzel. The moral of this story is, do not have a set schedule for conference day!

Creating a Successful Mentoring Program

Regardless of the level that students are achieving in your school, having a mentoring program in place will help close the achievement gap and support students that need extra help from adults in the building. I will go over how to identify students to be part of the mentoring program, how to structure the mentoring program, and how to maintain success throughout the year. Just like how you structure parent-teacher conferences, there is no correct way to do this, and your approach will vary based on data that you pull from your school. The key to a successful mentoring program is using data to make effective decisions that will help students at your school inside and outside of the classroom. I will go over a few "what no to do" scenarios that can hinder the implementation and progress of mentoring programs. I have been a part of many successful programs and many unsuccessful programs. In all of the programs I have been a part of, the leader set the tone for success, and it will ultimately be up to you to make your mentoring program successful.

Starting the Program

Creating or continuing a mentoring program during your first year in a leadership position may seem like a daunting task, but you can do it! Regardless of if you are a team leader or department chair, implementing a successful mentoring program should be part of your first year in some capacity. Some schools may already have a mentoring system in place, or you may have to create one from scratch. There is not a perfect model on creating a mentoring system because the needs of each school differ, and your school's needs will even be different than the needs of schools within your district. However, in this chapter I will delve into how to create and implement a successful mentoring program in a school. I will describe in-depth how to implement the mentoring program in a grade level. However, if you are planning on implementing a school-wide mentoring program, the structure I describe can be scaled to an entire school. When creating a mentoring program, ask yourself what problem you are trying to solve. Does your school struggle with literacy achievement? Does your school struggle with math achievement? Are there a lot of students that are frequently absent? Identifying a problem your school is facing will enhance the success of your mentoring program and its impact on the school.

Data, Data, Data

The first thing you need to do before making any decisions is to look at student achievement data. This needs to be done during the first week of school to ideally start helping students in need as soon as possible. Most school districts have software that allows you to pull student achievement data on literacy and math. Some states may have more metrics for you to analyze, but at minimum, literacy and math data will be made available. During the first week of school, I would pull literacy and math data to look for trends in the data and take detailed notes on these trends. I want to note, if you are a team leader, I would only look at the data for your grade level and if you are a department chair, you may need to look at the entire school's data. Again, for the purposes of this book, I am going to go in depth into a plan for a specific grade level. After looking at student achievement data for literacy and math, I would then pull up attendance data from the previous year to see which students are truant. I personally would recommend creating a criterion to narrow down how students are chosen for the program to target the students most in needs. For the purposes of this example, I am going to be very specific in the criteria I use to choose students. You can be as broad or specific as you would like, but make sure the number of students chosen matches up 1 to 1 with adults on your team (I will delve into this more later). If I were to create a criterion for a mentoring program at the average school, I would make the criteria the following: Students who are absent more than 6% of all school days, students who achieve at the bottom 20% of state testing for literacy, and students who achieve at the bottom 20% of state testing for math. Using this criterion will ideally narrow down your list of students significantly, but this will depend on your school.

After using a criterion for choosing students, you will need to make a list of students to be part of your mentoring program. I recommend putting all of their information and data into one spreadsheet to be organized and have all of their information in one place. This information will be needed to present to teachers and staff members that are part of the program as well. I would have the mentee's name, parents' or guardians' email address, parents' or guardians' phone number, homeroom teacher, attendance data, literacy achievement data, and math achievement data. Having everything on one page and not in an elaborate presentation will decrease your stress and take less time to create. In the past, I have seen leaders make elaborate presentations with this data, the mentee's picture, and other things that are great, but not a good use of time. Below in my example, you can see that having everything on one page is effective and has all of the information that you need.

Student Name	Parents' or Guardians' Email address	Parents' or Guardians' Phone number	Homeroom Teacher	Attendance Data	Literacy Achievement Data	Math Achievement Data

Figure 4.1 Data Sheet for Mentoring

Presenting Data to the Team or School

After collecting and analyzing data on students, I always ensure I show staff members the numbers and go through my thought process. I always make it a point to go over the specific metrics of the data and why I chose the metrics. After showing staff the data, I assign mentors to students. Always remember to make the assignments before the meeting and not during the meeting to decrease any chaos about the program. I personally would not recommend allowing staff members to choose their own mentee because it could lead to some students not being wanted as a mentee while some specific students will be very popular among staff. Letting staff members choose their mentee can lead to less than desirable discussions and issues, so I recommend avoiding this at all costs. I always ensure I assign a mentee to a teacher that they have, but there are rare cases where a mentor does not have the mentee as a student. Examples of this can be when administrators, counselors, or a staff development teacher is part of the program. I am a strong believer in having a mentoring program be 1 to 1 (mentor/mentee). After telling staff their mentee, you will then go over a letter to be sent home to all the parents and guardians of all mentees to notify them that their student is in a mentoring program. Too many times I have heard of mentoring programs not notifying home and parents or guardians being very upset that they were not informed of the program. Below is an example of a letter or email you can send home to the parents and guardians of the mentees. Many mentoring programs send elaborate letters home, but I do not believe that is necessary. A simple letter notifying home is sufficient.

Mentoring Letter to be sent home or emailed

Greetings Parents or Guardians of _____,

My name is Stephen Katzel and I am a Seventh Grade Team Leader at Joe Doe Middle School. For the 20XX-20XX school year, your child Jane Poe was selected to be part of our mentoring program. I will serve as Jane's mentor to help her with academics throughout the year. Please email me if you have any questions about the program at Stephen.X.XYZ@schooldistrict.com.
I look forward to working with your student to make it a successful year.

Sincerely,

Mr. Katzel

Monitoring and Leading the Mentoring Program Throughout the Year

Throughout the year, I would recommend having a whole-group mentoring event at least once a month. You can buy snacks and invite any of the administration to come to the event. I would recommend having this event during lunch so that the mentoring students do not miss any class time. During the event, I would recommend keeping it to fifteen minutes, and only use the whole group event to update everyone on the successes of the mentoring program. You may be wondering: how do I keep staff members accountable for being a mentor with fidelity? To keep staff accountable, I would have them fill out a grade sheet every two weeks with their mentoring student and go over short-term and long-term goals as well. I would ask that staff document this and bring it to a team meeting. This requires team leaders being on board to dedicate a team meeting to mentoring every two weeks. However, using team time for mentoring is important because it creates more staff buy-in to the program. Asking staff members to use their planning time on the mentoring program is not fair to them and will create resentment. Now you may be wondering, when will staff members meet with their mentee? I always advise having mentoring students meet up with their mentor during homeroom time. Most schools have homeroom each day or at least a few days a week. This would be a perfect time to have mentoring students meet with their mentors and get to work. While a mentor is with their mentee, the rest of their homeroom class can be working on a different activity or catching up on homework. I strongly advise not forcing staff members to all meet in the same room for mentoring more than once a month. If you always require staff to all be in the same room, you may appear like a "micromanager". To further staff buy-in of the program, I would also develop a survey asking two simple questions. What did we do well with the mentoring program for the 20XX-20XX school year? What can we improve in our mentoring program for the next school year? I want to note, I would allow staff the option to put their name on the survey or submit it anonymously.

Measuring the Success of the Mentoring Program

Tracking the success of the mentoring program will allow you to build on your success and make tweaks for the future. I always keep the baseline data that I have on the mentoring program and then analyze data at the end of the year to track the impact of the program on students. The figure below

Student Name	Attendance Data (Before Monitoring Program)	Literacy Achievement Data (Before Monitoring Program)	Math Achievement Data (Before Monitoring Program)	Attendance Data (After Monitoring Program)	Literacy Achievement Data (After Monitoring Program)	Math Achievement Data (After Monitoring Program)

Figure 4.2 Second Data Sheet for Mentoring

shows a few metrics that you can use to measure the success of the program. You can measure growth by comparing attendance data, math achievement data, and literacy achievement data from the start of the program to the end of the program. For example, student John Doe was in the 34th percentile for math before the mentoring program. After being part of the program for a year, he is now in the 50th percentile for math. Another metric you can measure can be total group averages. For example, before starting the mentoring program, all 30 students averaged an attendance rate of 91%. After being part of the mentoring program for a year, the 30 students had an average attendance rate of 97.5%. However, depending on your school, you may be able to get more data points. The point I am trying to get across is that the more data you have available, the easier it will be to track the success of your mentoring program.

Final Thoughts

Being a leader in the world of education will allow you to plan and implement important school-wide events and programs. Facilitating parent conferences is a pivotal moment in the school year that will allow you to reach out to the community at large and build a positive school culture. Parent conferences also enable you to help all students improve academically and/or socially by building a bridge between schools and homes. Developing a mentoring program at your school will ideally close the achievement gap and promote academic success among your most "at risk" students. Mentoring programs allows staff members to provide guidance to students that may need extra support in improving their attendance, math proficiency, or literacy proficiency. Creating a successful mentoring program will be the "feather in your cap" that solidifies winning your first year of leadership. The mentoring program exemplifies all of the leadership skills you have in your toolkit and allows for you to further your school's goals for the year.

5

Coaching Teachers

Conducting formal and informal observations throughout the year is part of being a school leader. Regardless of the experience level of the teachers you supervise, at the end of the day you are going to serve in a coaching capacity for them as well. Even if your position is not a supervisory role, at minimum you will be asked to help with informal observations of teachers. The feedback that you give teachers will vary based on their experience level and needs. Some new leaders will supervise experienced teachers while other new leaders will supervise novices. Knowing what to look for during observations and how to give feedback in an appropriate way is a key aspect of being an instructional leader. A couple topics and images in this chapter will overlap with my first book, which advises first year teachers on how to achieve a successful first year of teaching. However, this book is about educational leadership and will look at the images and topics through the lens of leadership in a completely different light than my first book.

Organize Long-Term Lesson Plans

As an instructional leader, you should have a grasp on what is occurring in the classrooms of the staff you supervise. However, I personally do not

DOI: 10.4324/9781003230274-6

recommend asking staff members to send you lesson plans for a variety of reasons. It is not a good use of time to look at dozens and dozens of lesson plans per week and you will come across as a "micromanager" if you ask for copies of plans. Instead of individual lesson plans, ask staff members to send you their quarterly planning guide. At the start of each quarter, I would recommend dedicating a team meeting, part of a staff meeting, or a department meeting to allow cohorts to develop a long-term planning guide for the quarter. For example, during the first department meeting of the year, Mr. Katzel (Department chair) allowed the Social Studies department to develop their long-term planning guide for quarter one. He now knows what the sixth-grade cohort, seventh-grade cohort, and eighth-grade cohort are teaching on each day of the quarter. Another recommendation that makes life easier for school leaders is to house all long-term planning documents in a cloud that each person on your team, department, or school can access. When you put the document in the cloud, this allows staff members to make real-time edits that you can also see immediately. If you do not use cloud services, this would require staff members to constantly email you new versions of the long-term planning sheet and would be annoying to deal with. By hosting everything in the cloud, you will make your life easier! Also, you will now know what to expect anytime you are conducting informal or formal observations. I will state an example using the planning sheets I created below. "Mr. Katzel is planning on conducting an informal observation of Mr. Doe's ninth grade History class on November 23rd. According to Mr. Doe's planning calendar, Mr. Katzel can expect Mr. Doe to be teaching about Warring City-States". If Mr. Katzel walks into Mr. Doe's classroom and sees him doing a picture analysis, Mr. Katzel now knows that Mr. Doe is a day behind on his planning calendar. If Mr. Katzel walks into Mr. Doe's class and he is doing a primary source analysis, Mr. Katzel now knows Mr. Doe is one day ahead of schedule. Having knowledge about either of these scenarios will allow Mr. Katzel to have a better grasp on what is occurring in the classrooms of the staff members that he supervises. If Mr. Katzel then conducts an informal observation of Mrs. Poe (the only other ninth grade History teacher at the school) he can see where Mrs. Poe is at on the planning guide and determine if the cohorts are aligned in planning or if they are teaching completely different things. Something as simple as having staff members create a long-term planning guide allows leaders to do their jobs more efficiently and effectively. I strongly believe this also serves as the first step to conducting formal and informal observations effectively.

	Sunday	Monday	Tuesday	Wednesday	Thursday	Friday	Saturday
Unit 2- Week #1	11/8	11/9 1 Citizenship in Ancient Times!	11/10 2 Citizenship in Ancient Times!	11/11 3 (Half Day) Purpose of Ancient Governments	11/12 4 Secondary Source Analysis	11/13 5 Purpose of Government (Secondary Source Analysis) HW #1	11/14
Unit 2- Week #2	11/15	11/16 6 Traits of Citizenship	11/17 7 Mapping Ancient Middle East	11/18 8 Ancient Civilizations	11/19 9 Map Quiz	11/20 10 (Half Day) Picture Analysis	11/21
Unit 2- Week #3	11/22	11/23 11 Warring City States	11/24 12 Primary Source Analysis HW #2	11/25 No School (Thanksgiving Break)	11/26 No School (Thanksgiving Break)	11/27 No School (Thanksgiving Break)	11/28
Unit 2- Week #4	11/29	11/30 13 Class Discussion: Choose a side in Ancient Times!	12/1 14 Class Discussion: Choose a side in Ancient Times!	12/2 15 Claim and Evidence Practice	12/3 16 Claim and Evidence Practice HW #3	12/4 17 Historical Essay Prep	12/5
Unit 2- Week #5	12/6	12/7 Science Education Field Trip (Entire 6th Grade)	12/8 Science Education Field Trip (Entire 6th Grade)	12/9 Science Education Field Trip (Entire 6th Grade)	12/10 Science Education Field Trip (Entire 6th Grade)	12/11 Science Education Field Trip (Entire 6th Grade)	12/12
Unit 2- Week #6	12/13	12/14 18 Historical Essay	12/15 19 Historical Essay	12/16 20 Historical Essay	12/17 21 Historical Essay	12/18 22 Historical Essay	12/19

Figure 5.1 The first six weeks of a long-term planning calendar.

Winter Break	12/20	12/21	12/22	12/23	12/24	12/25	12/26
	Winter Break (No School)	Winter Break (No School)	Winter Break (No School)	Winter Break (No School)	Winter Break (No School)	Winter Break (No School)	
Winter Break	12/27	12/28	12/29	12/30	12/31	1/1	1/2
	Winter Break (No School)	Winter Break (No School)	Winter Break (No School)	Winter Break (No School)	Winter Break (No School)	Winter Break (No School)	
Unit 2- Week #7	1/3	1/4 23 Inventions of the Ancient World	1/5 24 Impact of Technology HW #4	1/6 25 Social Class Analysis	1/7 26 Social Class Analysis	1/8 27 Impact of War	1/9
Unit 2- Week #8	1/10	1/11 28 Class Discussion: Art Analysis	1/12 29 Class Discussion: Art Analysis	1/13 30 Thesis Statement	1/14 31 Paragraph Activity- Thesis Statement Practice	1/15 32 Start of Rebellions	1/16
Unit 2- Week #9	1/17	1/18 No School (MLK Day)	1/19 33 Impact of Rebellions	1/20 34 Review Day	1/21 35 Test	1/22 36 Review Common Errors on Test	1/23
Unit 2- Week #10	1/24	1/25 37 Webquest	1/26 38 Webquest	1/27 39 Article Analysis	1/28 40 Article Analysis	1/29 41 (Half Day) Newspaper Article	1/30

Figure 5.2 The last four weeks of a long-term planning calendar.

Coaching Novice Teachers Versus Experienced Teachers

Informal and formal observations serve as an outlet to coach and develop the staff members that you supervise. The misconception in the education field or any professional field is that once you reach a certain point, you cannot improve your craft and reach the "glass ceiling". It doesn't matter if someone has been teaching for 20 months or 20 years, anyone in the education field can always get better in something, including myself! As a new leader in a building, do not only focus on helping novice teachers, look for ways to help experienced teachers as well. Typically, novice teachers will have different needs than experienced teachers, but it will vary by school. Areas that novice and experienced teachers typically struggle with are technology, classroom management, routines, and disorganization. In this chapter, I will delve into solutions to solve the problems I just mentioned. The root of most problems that occur in the classroom stem from disorganization and classroom management. Once teachers get organized and solve classroom management issues, their teaching capabilities will significantly increase.

The "One-Pager"

When conducting classroom observations of teachers, it may be difficult to identify the learning objective of the lesson. You may know the topic of the lesson if you have access to their long-term planning calendar, but some teachers struggle with identifying a learning objective for the day. Some teachers struggle with showing learning objectives to their students, which detracts from the lesson they are teaching. Other teachers struggle with classroom management during the first five minutes of class and when students walk in the door. It doesn't matter if you work at an elementary school or high school, student crave structure and if their teacher has different expectations for them every day when they walk in the door, behavioral issues will arise. If a teacher you supervise is struggling with classroom management during the beginning of class or telling their students the learning objective for the day, I highly recommend coaching them to make a one-pager each class period. As you see in the example below, there is the date, do now, homework, objective, and agenda. The "do now" tells students exactly what to do when they walk into the room, which would aide in helping teachers that struggle with behavior management. Also, having the objective on the board will remind the teacher to read it at some point during the class period. Another aspect of the one-pager takes away the dreaded questions of, when is the homework due?" "Is there homework tonight?" Something as small as having students constantly ask these questions and call out can throw off a teacher that struggles with classroom management. I would coach the teacher (and entire school for that matter) to use the acronyms of DD and DL when assigning homework or classwork. I would have the teacher explain to their class that "DD" stands for the due date or official day the assignment has to be turned in for full credit. The "DL" stands for the final day that a student can turn something in for partial credit. I could write an entire chapter on why having these acronymous school-wide would be beneficial, but I will keep it to the scope of an individual classroom. The one-pager aides teachers that are disorganized, making them more organized in their lesson plans and presentation to their classes. Disorganization at the beginning of class sets the tone for the rest of the class period. Coaching an experienced or novice teacher struggling with organization and management to create a one-pager each class period will ideally improve their teaching capabilities and highlight your abilities as an instructional coach.

Date: Tuesday, September 9, 2020

Do Now: Write down your homework and then start the warm up

Homework: Ancient Civilization Reading and Questions: DD- 9/11, DL: 9/18

Objective: SWBAT: describe the 8 themes of geography

Agenda: Warm Up -> Close Read -> 8 Themes of Geography Reading/Questions -> Interactive Exit Ticket

Figure 5.3 An example of a "one-pager".

Disorganization Leads to Problems, Organization Leads to Solutions

In my observations, it has become clearer each year that teachers who struggle the most are typically disorganized. Disorganization leads to stress and less effective teaching in the classroom for a variety of reasons. A teacher that is disorganized may spend the first 15 minutes of the day searching for their lesson plans and papers for the day. For this reason, I always advocate for disorganized teachers to start organizing their files so that they can easily locate their lesson plans each day. In fact, the system of organization I advocate for will allow teachers to easily find all of their files each year. Below you can see that I organized each file to align with the long-term lesson plan document that teachers create at the start of each quarter. Each file is numbered and labeled according to the day of the lesson and the unit. Having this level of organization leads to staff members being less stressed and better able to plan for the future. I am also confident that helping teachers attain this level of organization will lead to solutions to other problems they are having as an educator.

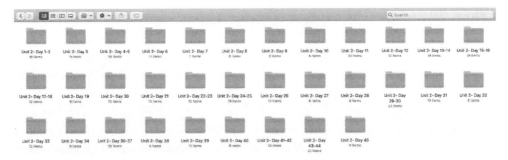

Figure 5.4 Folders that contain lesson plans and resources for a unit of study.

Peer Visits

Another strategy in coaching struggling and strong teachers is to set up peer visits among your team, department, or school. Peer visits can be as in-depth or not in-depth as you choose them to be. Some leaders like making peer visits very in-depth and have staff members fill out a long form after each visit. I see the logic behind this but would offer an alternative to having a long form. In my opinion, peer visits should serve a specific purpose and not feel like chore for other teachers to complete. I would create a sign-up list of staff members and only allow a teacher to be visited once. It would be very overwhelming to have five people visit one teacher's room in a week. After conducting the peer visit, I would then ask that staff members fill out a short survey that asks about the peer visit. When creating peer visits, ensure that there is a timeline sent out on the time frame for visits to occur as well. At minimum, I would share some highlights from the peer visits with your team, department, or staff about the peer visits. On a different note, if you are working with a struggling teacher, I highly suggest conducting one peer visit to a strong teacher's classroom. This allows a struggling teacher to see what methods and practices are making a colleague's classroom run smoothly.

PEER VISITS SIGN UP SHEET

Teacher Name	Date	Scheduled Visitor
Mr. Doe	3/18	Mr. Katzel
Mr. Katzel	3/21	Mrs. Poe
Mrs. Poe	3/23	Mr. T
Mr. T	3/25	Mr. Doe

Cohort Planning

Regardless of how your school is structured, it is important to ensure that cohort planning occurs! Cohort planning can involve two or more staff members that teach a specific subject matter and grade level, that follow the same curriculum. Or cohort planning can involve two or more staff members in different grade levels, but that all teach the same subject matter. I wanted to mention this format as well because some schools have only one teacher per subject, per grade level. I have heard of many K-8 schools having four teachers per grade level in sixth to eighth grade. Allowing for teachers in the same content matter to collaborate and bounce ideas off of each other will ideally help struggling and excelling teachers learn from each other. When working with teachers that are struggling, I always ask how their cohort planning is going. That simple question allows me to get a clear picture of who collaborative staff members are and how it impacts struggling teachers. For example, Mr. Doe is a struggling teacher that teaches sixth grade math. His cohort planning partner is Mr. Katzel, a teacher that excels in the classroom. However, Mr. Katzel is not willing to share lesson plan ideas with Mr. Doe because he does not want Mr. Doe to "steal" his work and ideas. Mr. Doe feels that he cannot ask his planning partner for help for anything outside of their quarterly planning calendar. Mr. Katzel is creating an unhealthy environment for collaboration and this needs to be addressed. I do want to mention, each planning cohort should have established guidelines to ensure that each member is contributing equally. One member should not be doing all of the work. In this case with Mr. Doe and Mr. Katzel though, a leader needs to meet with both and explain the importance of collaborating to ensure that all students in the grade level are receiving comparable experiences in both courses, since they are identical. To circle back to my initial point, if a teacher is struggling, asking about their cohort planning may lead you to discover potential problems, but also potential solutions. If you feel it is necessary, notify cohort members that you are planning on attending the next planning meeting to exchange ideas with them. It is important to frame the email through the lens that you are attending to exchange ideas. If you email a planning cohort, "I am coming to observe your cohort planning because of these reasons . . ." it will make you look like a micromanager. How you frame emails, it sets the tone for a meeting!

Lesson Plan Together

As an instructional leader, I find it very important to offer the chance to lesson plan with staff members that you supervise. Some staff members may feel neglected in their current team or may just want to hear a fresh perspective. I want to mention that if a staff member is struggling with lesson planning, definitely offer a time to plan with them! If a staff member is hesitant to plan with you, make sure you frame it was a collaborative meeting, not an evaluative one. New staff members or struggling staff members will be more apprehensive to plan with a school leader because they do not want the session to be a "Gotcha!" A "Gotcha" is when a school leader looks for chances and opportunities to get a person they supervise in trouble. There are numerous ways that a "Gotcha" can happen, but I will tell you one using planning as an example. "Mr. Z asked Mr. Doe to plan a lesson with him about history. Weeks later after conducting a formal observation of Mr. Doe, Mr. Z writes very negative things about Mr. Doe's planning methods and ideas". Mr. Z did not plan with Mr. Doe to help him as a teacher. Rather, he planned with him to look for things to hold over Mr. Doe's head later on. Leaders like Mr. Z are divisive and do not foster trust among their staff members that they supervise. In fact, leaders like Mr. Z do not promote student achievement and contribute to the fact that the average teacher only teaches for five years.

After planning a lesson with a teacher, always offer to go and observe the lesson or to have a discussion after they implement the lesson in their classroom. It is important that you tell them your observation or follow up discussion is non-evaluative. I would recommend offering a planning template to use when planning a lesson. In fact, I would recommend using my lesson plan template below for each lesson of the year. Teachers that struggle with lesson planning may have a difficult time visualizing how to allocate their time each class period. That is why I included a section for the agenda and an estimation of how long each task will take. Writing out prior learning allows teachers that struggle with planning to be reminded of what they have already gone over and allows them to further focus on the task at hand. Writing out the learning objective will ideally allow a teacher that struggles with planning to correlate their exit ticket or formative assessment to measure the learning objective. My sample lesson plan is a good starting point for struggling planners. You can make your lesson plans as detailed or descriptive as you would like.

Teacher: Mr. Katzel	**Grade/Subject:** Sixth Grade Social Studies	**Unit/Day of Unit:** Unit 1, Day 2
Periods: 1,2,3,6	**Previous Learning:** Analyzed maps of Europe, online mapping activities	**State Standard** human and physical characteristics by analyzing maps
Academic Vocabulary: Human Geography, Physical Geography, Human Characteristics, Physical Characteristics	**Daily Objective:** SWBAT (Students Will Be Able To) – Identify human and physical characteristics by analyzing maps and other secondary sources	**Essential Questions:** Why do maps change?
Warm Up/Introduction: Analyze a Map Worksheet	**Exit Ticket/ Summarization:** On the classroom portal, there will be a multiple choice exit car	**Lesson Timing (Estimation in Minutes)** 1. Warm Up (5) 2. Geography Close Read (5) 3. Map Analysis (15) 4. Secondary Source Analysis (15) 5. Review Secondary Source Analysis (5) 6. Exit Card (15)

Sample Lesson Plan: Sixth Grade Social Studies

Figure 5.5 Sample Lesson Plan: Sixth Grade Social Studies.

Encourage Balance, You Cannot Grade Everything!

If you are working with or coaching a teacher that is struggling, it is important to have a conservation on the amount of grading they are doing. The realities of being a teacher is grading takes up a lot of our time. Many new teachers think that they have to grade everything, which leads to bad consequences. Burning out, exhaustion, and disillusion all happen when a teacher is grading too much work. If a teacher has 150 students and grades five assignments a week, that will mean looking at 750 papers per week and writing feedback! Every district has grading minimums per week, but no district (that I have heard of) has a minimum of 5 assignments per week.

Encourage teachers that over-grade to look at assignments and give feedback in other ways. It can be something such as making two piles of work, separating students that met the learning objective and students that did not meet the learning objective. Another tip to tell teachers is to set time limitations on grading papers. Will students benefit more from getting a graded paper back 2–3 days early, but have an exhausted teacher the next day? Or will students benefit more from having a fully rested teacher in class and getting their graded work a few days later? I strongly believe that students will benefit from a well-rested teacher more than a teacher who is exhausted. Grading is important for teachers to do, but it should not be the most important thing that takes over successful teaching.

Assign a Mentor

Assigning a mentor to a struggling or new teacher gives a different level of support and leads to positive outcomes. I always recommend assigning a mentor teacher to a new teacher in the building. The mentor should not be a supervisor and be viewed more as a trusted adult for the teacher to go to for advice. Having a second person to go to for advice provides new teachers an outlet that is safe and non-evaluative. Ideally, the mentor teacher and new teacher will at minimum develop a work friendship, which also makes it easier for the new teacher to make friends at work. Obviously, we do not go into teaching to make friends, but when you become at least friendly with co-workers, it does make the work environment better. Sometimes new teachers are completely new to the area, state, or even country. Having a mentor helps ease the transition to the school. Struggling teachers can also benefit from having a mentor in a non-evaluative role. When a struggling teacher is provided a peer to collaborate with, they will ideally have a second outlet for ideas other than their supervisors. In a perfect world, team leaders, department chairs, and administrators would be all viewed as trusted people for struggling or new teachers to approach. But this is not the reality in some situations, and providing a mentor is a useful idea. I personally do not believe that a mentor needs to teach the same subject or grade level as the mentee. If you believe someone is a strong teacher and good influence, assign them to a mentee. If possible, see if there are school funds available to pay a stipend to teachers that mentor others. I do want to note, definitely be selective in who you allow to officially mentor others at your school. If a jaded teacher is mentoring a new teacher at your school, numerous issues can arise from this. The mentoring program at your school can be as informal or formal as you would like. However, having a mentoring program or initiative available to new or struggling teachers will ideally increase your teacher retention rate and lead to a more positive work climate.

Conducting Informal Observations

Conducting informal observations is an important part of being a new leader in a building. As a new leader, I always recommend conducting an informal observation of each teacher you supervise within the first month of school. Sending a quick email out to staff members notifying them that you will be visiting their classrooms throughout the first month of school will be appreciated by your staff members. As a new leader in your building, they are still feeling you out too! Giving notification of informal observations shows your staff members you are willing to communicate with them and give them notice when you are conducting walk-throughs. In addition, I would not recommend staying more than 15 minutes per informal observation so that you can visit everyone during the first month. After the first month of school, you don't have to announce that you will be conducting informal observations and they can be unannounced. I just believe in giving a heads up during the first month of school is always a good idea. Informally observing staff members that you supervise allows you to get a feel for their strengths and areas they can improve on. When conducting informal observations, make sure you do not cause a disruption when walking into the classroom and try to take a seat in the back. You do not want to distract students or the teacher and sitting in the back of the classroom will help achieve this.

After each observation, I highly recommend sending a quick follow up email to the teacher about the visit, so they are not left wondering about your impromptu visit. Below are two examples of emails that you can send after conducting an informal observation. One email is short, simple, and does not require any follow up from the teacher since the informal observation went smoothly. The second email can be sent after conducting an informal observation that did not go particularly well for a variety of reasons. It is possible the teacher struggled with classroom management, lesson implementation, or lesson structure. The email was not accusatory or harsh and was very specific in why you want to meet to follow up about the visit. To build a positive school culture, I also recommend sending out a weekly email to the entire school's staff highlighting a positive aspect of a visit in a teacher's classroom. Staff members doing good things should be recognized and people will appreciate that you are recognizing the good work of others. Sending a short blurb about the lesson and attaching a picture will build your credibility as a leader and improve staff morale.

Good Afternoon,

I sincerely enjoyed visiting your classroom this afternoon and seeing your lesson on ancient Greece. Students were actively engaged and asking intriguing questions. I also noticed that you provided students many opportunities to engage in discourse and share their ideas. I look forward to visiting your room again!

Thank You,

Mr. Katzel

Good Afternoon,

I enjoyed visiting your classroom this afternoon and seeing your lesson on ancient Greece. Students were actively engaged and asking intriguing questions. There were a few questions I had about the lesson and want to follow up about. Can we meet during your planning period tomorrow or on Friday? Please let me know which one is better for you.

Thank You,

Mr. Katzel

Conducting Formal Observations

Conducting formal observations in an effective manner are a key part of being a school-based leader and winning your first year. When conducting formal observations, it is important to follow the guidelines of your school district to ensure you are evaluating staff members in accordance with the district's standards. Depending on your school district's rules, you may be allowed to meet with a staff member before conducting an observation. If you are allowed to meet with a staff member before an observation, I would recommend having the meeting so that you can learn more about the upcoming lesson. If you are not able to have a meeting before the observation, I would recommend looking at their long term planning calendar, so you have an idea on what topic they are teaching. Another aspect of formal observations is they can be announced or unannounced. Again, this depends on how your school district conducts formal observations. Some school districts allow for formal observations to be announced while others do not. Looking into the rules around this will allow to be aware of how you can conduct formal observations. Regardless of the structures that your district has for formal observations, make sure that you take notes during your observation and always have a meeting with the teacher that you observed within a week of conducting the observation. If the observation didn't go well and a tough conversation needs to happen, make sure you go into the meeting with data. It can be really easy to seem critical of staff members when it sounds like you are stating an opinion and not a fact. For example, if you stated, "Students were not engaged during the warm up". This sounds like an opinion that can be argued with. Instead, you can say "During the warm up, five students had their head down and were not engaged with your presentation". The second sentence uses data to make a point and does not sound like an opinion or a "gotcha".

Final Thoughts

Coaching experienced and struggling teachers is part of being an instructional and effective leader. When you supervise staff members, they will all be at different parts of their careers and have different needs. Effectively coaching staff members under your supervision will not only promote student achievement but also a positive school culture. Recognizing that disorganization is the root of many teacher's struggles will allow you to make transformational change at your school. Once disorganized staff members become organized, they will be able to structure lesson plans, find their files, and plan long-term with ease. Working with novice and experienced teachers on how to get organized will be a game changer and allow others to excel as educators. Allowing staff members to conduct peer visits allows teachers to show the good work they are doing with collogues and further promotes student achievement and a positive school culture. Coaching is not ever going to be an easy thing to do, but you are now ready to take on the challenges that come with being a coach to other educators.

6

Interviewing for Your Next Role

The reality of any occupation is that you will most likely change roles at some point throughout the course of your professional career. In an ideal world, educators can stay at their current school for however long they desire without any outside forces changing that plan. However, that is not the reality and being unprepared for change will leave you significantly more overwhelmed than those who recognize that change can happen in an instant in the world of education. School districts can force teachers to involuntary transfer to another school for a variety of reasons. Funding can get cut, which leads to schools having less staff, which leads to staff members being transferred to a different school within the district. The point I am trying to make is that outside forces may lead you to have to change schools or even districts for a variety of factors. For personal reasons, you may have to move out of state and start applying for jobs outside of your comfort zone. Being professionally prepared for whatever life has to throw at you will ideally allow you to apply and interview for jobs with ease. Having a resume, cover letter, and artifacts are a large part of being prepared for your next role. In this chapter, I will go over tips and tricks I have learned over the years interviewing for positions and how I prepare myself for potential changes that may pop up in the future.

Updating Your Resume

The first thing I always recommend in preparing for any "unseen change" is for leaders to update their resume with their current job roles and title. If you

DOI: 10.4324/9781003230274-7

ever get a dreaded email that you are going to be involuntary transferred or have to move for personal reasons, having your resume ready to go will ease any burdens you may be facing. If you are stuck on what to put on your resume or how to update your qualifications, go to your district's website and look at the specific job qualifications that they listed for your position online. Using your district's qualifications as basis, update your resume to make it specific to your job roles. In addition to using your school district's qualifications, look up comparable school districts nearby to see what they listed for similar roles. This gives you multiple sources of information to look at while structuring your resume. In my opinion, there is not a perfect format when making a resume that demonstrates instructional leadership. However, the following guidelines should be considered when creating a new resume or updating an existing one. Do not make your resume over two pages! I have seen countless educators submit resumes that are three or four pages long which did not do them any favors. Employers will have dozens or even hundreds of resumes to go through for specific openings. Making your resume concise will be appreciated and get you to stand out more. The second piece of advice I have is to check for any spelling or grammatical errors. Spelling and grammatical errors make candidates look bad and portray the candidate as not careful in crafting important documents. The third piece of advice I always give to educational leaders, is to highlight your achievements. Too many people are afraid of coming across as brash or arrogant. Remember, your resume is selling you to an employer! They need to know all of your accomplishments and achievements to determine if they want to extend an interview. To further discuss this topic, make sure your accomplishments highlight actionable things you have done, and not just degrees. Listing your degrees and certifications is important but these should not be the only accomplishments that you list. Listing your GPA (grade point average) from college or grad school is okay but will not separate you from other candidates. Just like not listing your GPA from college or grad school will not really hurt your chances either. School districts care more about the degrees, and less about the GPA of the candidates that they are evaluating.

Building a Portfolio and Artifacts

In addition to updating your resume, it is important to keep a portfolio of artifacts that exemplifies all of the good work that you have accomplished over the years. When applying for leadership positions, many interviews require you to present and discuss specific artifacts that show the interviewers your capabilities. I always recommend creating an online portfolio and not keeping paper copies in order to maintain easy accessibility. I could not imagine keeping a paper portfolio instead of having a portfolio full of artifacts in the cloud. To clarify the difference between portfolios and artifacts, a portfolio is a collection of artifacts that exemplify your work throughout the course of your career. Artifacts can be a variety of things that highlight your leadership capabilities as well. An example of an artifact is a collection of documents that you created for your school's Magnet Showcase. The documents include the letters sent out to the community, schedule for the night, and picture of the event. Other examples of an artifact could be work that you have completed for a school committee or a professional development that you administered. Below, I posted an example of an artifact that can be part of a collection. The artifact is a one-pager that teachers can use during parent-teacher conferences. Something as simple as this document can easily be discussed and highlighted to talk about the strengths of a potential candidate. The example artifact below would allow me to start talking about the importance of providing families with a document that summarizes the meeting and also how I presented this document to my team. Something as simple as effectively discussing an artifact can change the entire outcome of an interview. In conclusion, keeping a portfolio will prevent you from having to scramble to put together documents if you are ever asked to present artifacts when applying for jobs.

Teacher: Mr. Katzel, Sixth Grade Team Leader & Social Studies	Email: step hen.X.XXX xxx@_____ ___.com	School Phone: 209-XXX-xxxx	Student Name: John Doe	OI Grade: 92% *(A)* Formative Grade Percentage – 90% Summative Grade Percentage –
				95% Homework Grade Percentage – 100% Essay Grade Percentage – 90%
Strengths 1. Asks for help/ clarification 2. Comes to class on time 3. Comes prepared with materials	**Area(s) to Discuss** 1. Turning in homework on time	**Action Steps for Success** 1. Weekly check-in from Mr. Katzel by email 2. Check assignments on the online portal	**Action Steps for Success** 3. Write down the homework each day in the student planner	**Notes:**

Figure 6.1 Sample resource that can be used for a parent-teacher conference.

Preparing for an Interview

When you are preparing for an interview, it is important to prepare in a manner that will set you up for success and equip you with specific talking points. Make sure that you know your resume extremely well and be prepared to answer questions about your resume. I have been part of interviews where the interviewers literally read through my resume and asked me questions about each section. Luckily, I studied my resume beforehand and know the contents of it very well, so I did not get tripped up. If I blanked on an answering a question about a specific part of my resume, it would have looked like

I embellished that detail. Nothing turns off potential employers more than having an applicant who lies about their credentials or accomplishments on a resume. After being comfortable with your resume, study two or three artifacts that you have in your portfolio to use as talking points to incorporate into your answers throughout the interview. Practicing talking about your resume and artifacts with a trusted adult before the interview will give you practice talking about them when you are in an interview.

In addition to studying your resume and familiarizing yourself with artifacts to talk about, make sure you do not get caught up in your credentials and certifications. While a lot of jobs require a certain degree or certificate, the interviewers already know which certifications and degrees you have because they already reviewed your resume. Throughout an interview, never state that your degree or certification is a reason for being able to do a specific job. Instead, focus on the experiences and ideas you developed while obtaining that specific degree or certification as an example of why you are a fit for the role. Too many people get caught up in accolades and pieces of paper without being able to convey the important aspects of why they are a fit for a specific leadership role. As cliché as it sounds, the ability to tell a story behind your experiences and being able to tie those experiences in a meaningful way to the interview questions will be able to set you apart from other applications for future roles. In some instances, I even find it helpful to write out responses to potential interview questions to prepare for an interview. You may find it helpful as well! Below are a few sample interview questions that I have seen and heard the most throughout my career.

SAMPLE INTERVIEW QUESTIONS

1. Tell us about your leadership experiences and how you got here today.
2. What is your biggest weakness as an educator and instructional leader?
3. What separates you from other candidates?
4. What is the most important trait of effective leaders?
5. How would you describe your leadership style?

Doing Research Before the Interview

Before I am scheduled to take part in an interview as a candidate, I always make sure to look up the school district and the school. When looking up both the school district and the school, I always look to find their values, mission statement, morals, and initiatives. Conducting research on these topics allows me to learn more about who is interviewing me and also gives me things to talk about during the interview. Before most interviews, you will usually be given a time frame into how long you are allocated to answer questions and potentially ask questions. If you are allotted thirty minutes, but your interview is over in less than ten minutes, you did not sell yourself enough or do enough talking! Knowing a school's mission statement will allow you to make connections with your own background and what the school values. For example, if continuous improvement is mentioned within a school's mission statement, you should make it a point to mention how your work aligns with the mission statement. Then you could easily talk about how you have always looked to continuously improve throughout the course of your career. In addition, it shows that you have conducted research into the school as well.

Controlling the Narrative for Role-Playing Interview Questions

During many interviews for leadership positions, schools like to have candidates partake in a role-play scenario to evaluate their critical thinking skills. Many people dread being part of these scenarios, but I thoroughly enjoy it! My mindset for partaking in role-playing scenarios during interviews it to take control of the narrative and keep the interviewers on their toes. I want to stress that it takes practice to be able to control of the direction of role-playing interview questions, but my tips will help you do to this! The first thing I decide before going into every interview is the names I will use for any role-playing interview question. I would recommend the names of your parents, siblings, or children so that you can easily remember them during the scenario. Another tip is to not let the person or people you are in the fake scenario with take complete control of the situation! It is important to introduce relevant variables to your responses which will ultimately keep your interviewers on their toes and allow you to demonstrate the ability to think critically and handle difficult situations. Below is an example of a role-playing scenario that could be asked during an interview and how my responses would dictate the direction of the question.

Interview Question

Two students got in an altercation in the lunchroom. The student that was responsible is in your office. What conversation would you have with the student? What consequences would you implement? The interviewer will play the role of the student, John Doe. Stephen will play the role of the school leader handling the situation.

> Stephen: Hello, John. Can you please tell me what happened in the lunchroom?
>
> John: Nothing happened in the lunchroom, I don't know what you are talking about! You are always out to get me!
>
> Stephen: John, I am not out to get you. I heard there was an incident in the lunchroom that were involved in. I have written statements from four students who said that you pushed Bill into a wall because he took your snack. The four students are Bill, Chris, Ali, and Matthew. Your written statement is much different, would you like to revise it?
>
> John: Fine, he took my snack and I pushed him.
>
> Stephen: Thank you for being honest, John. In alignment with the Code of Conduct for our school district, when a student puts hands on another student, they have to serve a lunch detention and call their parents or guardians.

The above scenario is an abbreviated example of how I would respond to an interview question that involved a role-playing scenario. Notice that I introduced a few different aspects to my responses to guide the conversation where I wanted it to go. Nowhere in the question did it mention written reports or the student code of conduct. I introduced this aspect into my replies to guide the conversation where I wanted it to go and ideally keep my interviewer on their toes. I was able to flip the script on them and ended up with a resolution at the end of the conversation! The four names I mentioned in my replies were predetermined before the interview so I would be able to mention them with consistency and not stumble. Again, these skills take practice, but you will get the hang of it in no time!

Approaching Job Fairs

If you ever have to attend job fairs, it is important to come prepared for the event so that you are using your time efficiently. Make at least 100 copies of your resume before going to the job fair. Some schools may only want one copy of your resume and some schools may want five copies of your resume to give to all of their administration. Having too many copies of your resume is better than having too few copies! Also, write down the names of the people you interviewed you so you can email them a follow-up thank you. This tip also applies to any interview in general. However, if you cannot find all of the email addresses of the interview panel, I would recommend emailing the principal and asking them to also thank the rest of the panel. Depending on the size of the job fair it can be overwhelming to candidates. Try to go into the job fair with specific schools and positions that you have in mind so that you can focus easier and not become overwhelmed with the options presented to you.

Final Thoughts

As great as it would be to stay at the same school for decades at a time, this typically is not feasible for a variety of reasons. Lack of opportunities for a promotion, involuntary transferring, lack of district funding, or life events may require you to change school districts or schools. Having an updated resume at all times will allow you to be better prepared for any potential changes in the future. Having a portfolio of artifacts that highlight your capabilities will also ease any potential hardships when applying for new roles. Conducting your own research into schools or districts will allow you to be prepare for interviews and make connections with any future employers. After reading this chapter, you will be ready to ace any interview that may come up in the future!

7

Case Studies on Handling Difficult Situations

Throughout your career as an educator, you are going to be faced with difficult situations that test your leadership skills and patience. In fact, any profession that involves constant communication with other adults creates situations and constructs that may be difficult to navigate. As an instructional leader, you are going to face unique challenges during your first year. In addition to being in a new position, you will have to learn how to approach conflict and difficult situations in an effective manner to effectively lead and interact with other leaders in the school. Throughout my time as a leader, I have made countless mistakes in dealing with situations and supervising educators. Although I have made many mistakes over the years, I always take ownership of my actions and decisions, which has allowed me to continue being an effective leader. I am a strong believer in that it is not about the mistakes that you make as a leader, it is how you respond to your mistakes. Taking accountability for your actions involves apologizing and having a dialogue with people. All of this is related to interpersonal connections that you have to maintain at work with different groups of people. In this chapter, I am going over examples of difficult situations that you may face as an instructional leader. I could honestly write an entire book on difficult situations that you will face, how you can respond, how you should respond, and the positive or negative consequences of responding a specific way. However, I value your time and will plan on focusing on specific situations that I believe will likely arise during your first year in a leadership position. Even if you get a leadership position in a school that you have worked at for years, the dynamic

DOI: 10.4324/9781003230274-8

of many of your work relationships can change. My goal is for you to walk away from this chapter with a sense of determination about taking on difficult events as a new leader. Preparing yourself for potentially difficult situations, meetings, interactions, and conversations will allow you to win your first year of leadership.

Case Studies

Case Study 1 – Your Voice Has Not Been Heard by Other Leaders for the Past Four Committee Meetings

Scenario

You are a new leader in a school and have been assigned to the Scheduling Committee. You have just completed your third meeting with two other leaders in your school and are feeling very frustrated with how the meetings have been going. Mrs. E and Mr. O are on the leadership team with you and attend all of the same meetings as well. Also, everyone on the committee has the same job title. Throughout the course of the last three meetings, Mrs. E and Mr. O have spoken over 80% of the time during the meetings and have not been considerate with their speaking time. In addition, when you try to speak up during meetings and voice your ideas, they both interrupt you without apologizing. Both Mrs. E and Mr. O have been at your school for decades and are established leaders. In addition, Mrs. E and Mr. O are family friends outside of work. You just entered your fourth committee meeting and are very frustrated because of the previous meetings. The fourth committee meeting just finished and you want to voice your concerns. How should you approach this situation?

Response

Being an instructional leader requires tact and patience when working with people that aren't respectful of hearing other opinions. The reality of any job is that you will work with people that are difficult to collaborate and plan with. Approaching Mrs. E and Mr. O in a respectful manner is extremely important because you are on the same committee with them. If you get angry and lash out, your working relationships with Mrs. E and Mr. O will be damaged and working on the same committee will be difficult. At the end of the fourth meeting, I would ask Mrs. E and Mr. O if we could chat for a few minutes. I would state, "I have enjoyed working on the same committee with both of you and have learned a lot. In the first few meetings, it was a bit difficult to voice my opinions and I was interrupted a few times. For future meetings, I would appreciate the chance to contribute to the discussions equally and increase my participation in the discussion". Notice that my response is respectful, and states the problem and solution to the problem in a concise statement. If I lashed out and told Mrs. E and Mr. O that they talked too much, the chances of a productive discussion about my concerns would be slim to none. Being mindful of your to approach conflict will save you a lot of time and heartache in the future. If you feel that your voice is not being heard by colleagues, respectfully discuss solutions with your colleagues about concerns. Not having discussions also leads to resentment and the increased likelihood that you will start dreading specific meetings with specific people. Being proactive to concerns will ideally increase your participation in committees and your ability to collaborate with other leaders in your building.

Case Study 2 – A Direct Report Does Not Like You Because They Interviewed for Your Job

Scenario

You just started your first day at your new school. Throughout the day, you have introduced yourself to numerous colleagues and have had conversations with them. Toward the end of the day, you see a teacher that you have not met, and you go up to them to introduce yourself. After saying hello, the teacher looks at you and promptly walks away. Another colleague (Mr. Bremer) witnesses the interaction and informs you that Mr. Doe interviewed against you for the team leader position. Mr. Bremer also tells you that Mr. Doe has wanted the position for years and has been at the school for over 15 years now. In the next few days, Mr. Doe avoids you and is very cold when he is in the same room as you. For better or for worse, Mr. Doe is a math teacher, and you are responsible for observing and coaching math teachers that school year. In addition, Mr. Doe has been teaching for 30 years and you are 30 years old yourself. Mr. Doe has children that are older than you and you are his direct supervisor. How should you approach this situation?

Response

The realities of applying for jobs and interviewing can be harsh and difficult for many people. Mr. Doe has been at the school for 15 years and expected that his seniority would get him hired. In addition, Mr. Doe is very upset that a younger candidate got hired over him because he felt that he has "put in his dues" at the school. The best way to handle this situation is to continue to greet him when you cross paths and to always act professional, even if Mr. Doe does not. There can be a lot of factors at play that you are completely unaware of once you arrive at a school. Many schools and staff members have complex histories that you are not a part of but can be affected by. Since Mr. Doe is a direct report, you are going to have to conduct classroom observations and interact with each other. He may lash out and be irrational when dealing with you out of jealousy. The best way to handle your interactions with Mr. Doe would be to always have data after observations, leaving less room for disagreement. For example, do so if you conducted a classroom observation and then met with him to give feedback. I would not recommend phrasing a statement that seems like an opinion, "Mr. Doe, your calling practices need to be more balanced". This statement could easily be disputed without having data present. Framing the feedback with data is more impactful. "Mr. Doe, in the 30-minute observation I conducted, you posed 10 questions to the class and called on three students to answer all 10 of the questions". Having data included in our interactions with Mr. Doe will leave less room for disagreement. Another tip in interacting with him is just to remain patient. Over time, his anger and resentment for not getting your job will ideally cool down. By always being professional around Mr. Doe he would ideally eventually be able to view your working relationship in a positive way.

Case Study 3 – You Disagree With a Decision That Your Boss Made

Scenario

Mrs. Doe is a principal in their first year at your school and new to your school district. During the first leadership meeting, Mrs. Doe outlines the schedule for teachers when they come back the week before school starts. Over 80% of the time during the week is either meetings or professional development sessions for teachers. The other 10% of the allocated time is for the sixth-grade orientation. Only 10% of the week is allocated to teacher planning time, which is less than half of the allocated planning time from last year's pre-service week. Mrs. Doe ends the meeting before any other leaders can address the lack of planning time. Do you say something before people walk out the door? Do you say anything at all at a later time?

Response

The reality of any job is that you are not always going to agree with your bosses on decisions that they make. At the end of the day, you have to respect the decisions your bosses make and implement them. However, voicing your opinion and ideas in a respectful manner is okay if you approach it the correct way. If you disagreed with Mrs. Doe in front of the entire leadership team, she may have viewed this as you trying to grandstand her or trying to show her up to the leadership team. The reality is that you both are new to your school, so you have no repertoire since it is the summer before school. Also, Mrs. Doe is new to the school district, so she may not be familiar with district policies. The best way to handle the situation is to request a brief meeting with Mrs. Doe either at the end of that day or the following day. In the meeting, you can state alternatives to the initial plan with limited teacher planning time. In addition, you should present a sample schedule that includes more planning time and explain why giving teachers more time to plan and cohort plan is important. Approaching Mrs. Doe in a one-on-one meeting gives you a better chance of having your voice heard and decreases the chance of potential conflicts. Having a solution to the problem greatly helps your cause. Whenever people go to bosses with problems but no solutions, it makes them look like they are just complaining. When you go to a boss with a problem and a solution, it makes you look proactive and like you are able to take initiative in solving issues at the school. Even if a boss does not take the advice or adopt the plan you present, they will be more inclined to seek your feedback since you approached them in a respectful way, identified a problem, and developed a solution.

Case Study 4 – A Co-Worker Constantly Makes Comments on Your Clothes and Appearance

Scenario

Mr. Doe is your direct report and has made a few interesting comments about your clothing and appearance throughout the first month of school. The comments haven't been completely rude, but they still have been strange. Comments such as "Your sweater does not match your pants" or "I noticed you got a haircut; it was an interesting choice". After discussing these comments with a trusted co-worker, Mr. Katzel was informed that Mr. Doe makes these types of comments to other people as well and has not been disciplined for this in the past. How should you handle this situation?

Response

Being a supervisor requires you to handle difficult situations with poise. Having poise is a combination of being able to have empathy for all involved parties but being able to guide the conversation where it needs to go. If you do not address Mr. Doe's comments, he will continue to make them directed towards your appearance throughout the year. The first thing I would do is document the behavior in a private folder and put down exactly what happened when he made the first comments. For example, "9/28, Mr. Doe made a comment about my sweater. 10/19, Mr. Doe made a comment about my haircut". Documenting the behavior will allow you to give specific dates and instances that the comments were made in case Mr. Doe denies the behavior.

The second thing I would do is schedule a meeting with Mr. Doe through an email. During the meeting, start with thanking him for meeting with you and be direct, in a respectful way. You can state, "Over the last few weeks, you made a few comments about my appearance that made me uncomfortable. I would appreciate it if you could be mindful about not making comments on my clothing and haircuts". Ideally, Mr. Doe would apologize, the behavior would stop, and you both can move forward with a positive professional relationship. If Mr. Doe denies saying the statements, then you can pull out your notes to give specific dates with the comments. Whenever I have to have difficult conversations with staff members, I always ensure I have data present to validate my points. I would not recommend debating whether he made the statements after pulling out your notes. I would recommend ending the meeting and stating, "Although we disagree with events, I would appreciate you being mindful of your comments about any staff members appearance. I want to move forward from this and look forward to having a great rest of the year". Ideally, Mr. Doe's comments will stop after this and no other issues will arise. If other issues arise, keep documenting the behavior and consult with your principal on next steps.

Case Study 5 – A Direct Report Adds You on Social Media and You Do Not Feel Comfortable Accepting the Friend Request

Scenario

After your first month of school, you have established positive work relationships with colleagues and staff that report directly to you. At the end of the week, you open up your social media to scroll and notice that a person that you supervise added you on social media. Doing the proper thing, you leave the request as pending, with no plans of accepting it or denying it because you still do not know the person. In the copy room on Monday, Mr. Doe approaches you to start a conversation. At the end of the conversation he asks, "Did you get my friend request?" How should you respond to Mr. Doe?

Response

Anytime social media is involved, I always recommend taking the cautious approach. I would highly recommend not adding any colleagues or direct reports on social media throughout the first year at your school. The reality of social media is that it usually contains very personal information and an intimate look into your life. Separating your personal life and work life is very important, and you do not want to intermix the two during your first year in a new role. I made the mistake of allowing colleagues to add me on social media and came to regret it. I took personal time off to take a long weekend trip, and I had people ask me about it when I got back on Monday. I was not thrilled that they brought it up and did so in a way that was condescending. If you feel comfortable adding someone on social media, by all means do so. However, be ready for people to learn more about you than you would like. In the situation described above, I would be very direct with Mr. Doe. I would state, "Hey Mr. Doe, I did get your friend request and glad that you brought it up. I have a personal policy that I do not add colleagues on social media for a variety of reasons. I appreciate your understanding on this!" My answer to Mr. Doe is direct and informs him that you do not want to add colleagues on social media. It makes your perspective clearly heard and is not rude in anyway.

Final Thoughts

Being an instructional leader requires you to be adaptive to difficult situations and not reactive. Just like in any professional industry, working any type of job is going to include some sort of conflict and difficult interpersonal situations that arise over time. How you react to difficult people and difficult situations will help shape your leadership capabilities and legacy as an instructional leader. I was purposeful in the five scenarios that I choose to discuss for a variety of reasons. I could write an entire book on difficult situations that could arise in a workplace but spending too much time on hypothetical situations would detract from the rest of the book. I wrote this chapter with the intention of you being mindful that difficult situations arise, and you must always be ready to handle them in a professional way. I always recommend staying calm in difficult situations and being reflective in whatever may happen. Educational leadership is a learning process that never ceases, always remember this!

Conclusion

Make it a Great Year!

Being in a leadership position is no easy task! Students, staff, and the community are all looking to make important decisions, promote student achievement, coach staff members on best practices, make data-driven decisions, conduct problem solving – and that's just in the morning! Throughout the school year, stay consistent in your words, actions, and commitment to making your school a better place for students, staff, and the community. With a winning system in place, you will be organized in every aspect of your role, you will have the tools to proactively solve problems, and you will be able to respond to the needs of your school with ease. Effective instructional leaders will help increase the average amount of time the person spends as an educator. The burn-out rate for teachers is currently at five years and the lasting impact of our teacher shortages are devastating. Strong leaders help aide strong teachers to deliver instruction and help students. Please use this book as a toolkit to refer to as a resource throughout your first year in a leadership position. You are going to do an amazing job and win your first year of educational leadership!

DOI: 10.4324/9781003230274-9

Appendix A

Monday	Tuesday	Wednesday	Thursday	Friday
August 2	August 3	August 4	August 5	August 6
1. Pre-Send an email to Mr. Doe about formal observation	1. Send email with data collection form for "Kid Talk"	1. Analyze Kid Talk data before the meeting	1. Team Meeting during fourth period	1. Send out weekly agenda to staff for upcoming week
2. Observe Seventh Grade Science	2. Meet with other department leaders for upcoming visit for high school enrollment	2. Team Meeting during fourth period	2. Draft weekly agenda for the week of August 9	2. Parent-Teacher Conference at 12:00 for Student John Doe
3. Send feedback to observed teacher	3. Analyze most recent state test scores for Math	3. Observe Seventh Grade Social Studies Cohort	3. Leadership Meeting at 4 pm	3. Cheek observation schedule for following week
4. Sync events to cell phone calendar	4. Sync events to cell phone calendar	4. Sync events to cell phone calendar	4. Sync events to cell phone calendar	4. Sync events to cell phone calendar

Figure 1.1 Personal Calendar – August 20XX

Appendix B

6th grade meeting at 9AM in room 156

Thursday, Aug 20, 2020
from 10 AM to 11 AM

9 AM	Opening week meeting tomorrow
10 AM	Record town hall at team meeting
	6th grade meeting at 9AM in room 156
11 AM	
Noon	

Calendar	● Calendar >
Alert	At time of event >

Delete Event

Appendix C

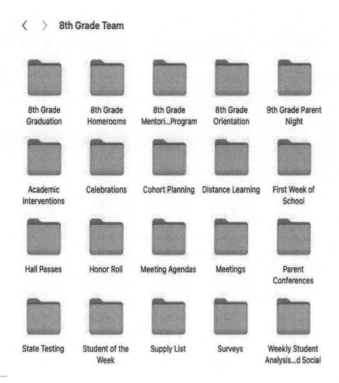

Appendix D

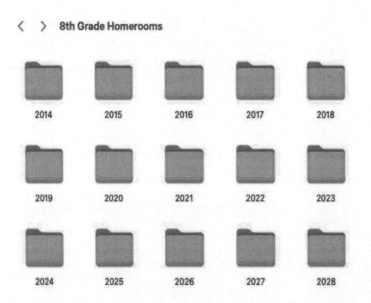

Appendix E

Sixth Grade Team Weekly Agenda

School Logo

Team Meeting Information – Room XXX from 2:00–2:30

Monday 3/15	Tuesday 3/16	Wednesday 3/17	Thursday 3/18	Friday 3/19
No Team Meeting – Content Area Planning	Team Meeting – Student Analysis	Team Meeting – Professional Development	Team Meeting – Data Analysis	No Team Meeting – Content Area Planning

Important Dates:

1. 3/23 – Professional Day for Teachers
2. 3/30 – Progress Reports are due at 3:00
3. 4/1 – Start of Spring Break
4. 4/10 – End of the marking period

Roles:

1. Timekeeper –
2. Task Manager –
3. Notetaker –

Appendix F

20XX-20XX
Observations
2 Items

Social Studies
Department
7 Items

Appendix G

Appendix H

Appendix I

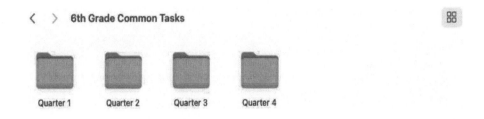

6th Grade Common Tasks

Quarter 1   Quarter 2   Quarter 3   Quarter 4

Appendix J

 20XX-20XX Observations

Observation Form
& Checklist

Teacher
Observa...Grid.pdf

Appendix K

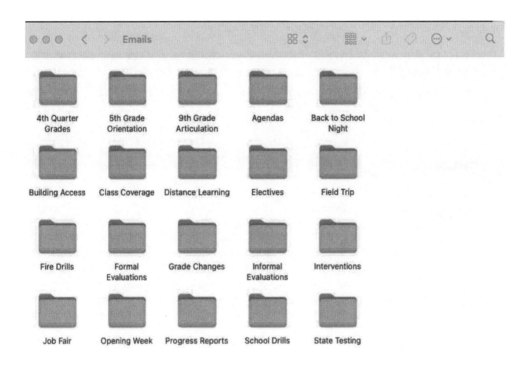

4th Quarter Grades	5th Grade Orientation	9th Grade Articulation	Agendas	Back to School Night
Building Access	Class Coverage	Distance Learning	Electives	Field Trip
Fire Drills	Formal Evaluations	Grade Changes	Informal Evaluations	Interventions
Job Fair	Opening Week	Progress Reports	School Drills	State Testing

Appendix L

Sixth Grade Data Analysis PD

Part #1 – Data Analysis

1. What percentage of our student population is . . .

   Male –
   Female –

2. What percentage of our student population is . . .

   ESOL (English as a Second Language) –
   FARMS (Free & Reduced Lunch) –
   Receive Special Education Services (IEP or 504 Plan) –

3. What percentage of our student population is . . .

   African American –
   American Indian –
   Asian –
   Caucasian –
   Hawaiian/Pacific Islander –
   Hispanic –
   Multiracial –

4. What percentage of our sixth graders have been absent in the last 10 days? (Please average the numbers).

Appendix M

	DATA CRUNCH	
Out of 1,000 students . . . 51 students have limited English language proficiency at our school. A school with a similar number of students in our district would have an average 187 students with limited English proficiency, Or . . . roughly 4 times the number of LEP students at our school.	Out of 1,000 students . . . We have 100 FARMS students at our school. A school with a similar number of students in our district has an average 401 students classified as FARMS, Or . . . roughly 4 times the number of FARMS students at our school.	Out of 1,000 students . . . We have 70 students receiving special education services at our school. A school with a similar number of students in our district would have on average of 150 students receiving special education services, Or . . . roughly double the number of students receiving special education services at our school.

Appendix N

Sixth Grade Data Analysis PD

Part #2 – Data Analysis

1   What percentage of our student population is . . .

Male – 49.1%
Female – 50.9%

2. What percentage of our student population is . . .

ESOL (English as a Second Language) – 5.1%
FARMS (Free & Reduced Lunch) – 10.1%
Receive Special Education Services (IEP or 504 Plan) – 7%

3. What percentage of our student population is . . .

African American – 12%
American Indian – 1%
Asian – 15%
Caucasian – 20%
Hawaiian/Pacific Islander – 4%
Hispanic – 46%
Multiracial – 2%

4. What percentage of our sixth graders have been absent in the last 10 days? (Please average the numbers).

5.7%

5. What data points surprised your group?

6. What school initiatives can be developed to increase attendance in sixth grade?

Appendix O

Student Name	Parent/ Guardians Email address	Parent/ Guardians Phone number	Homeroom Teacher	Attendance Data	Literacy Achievement Data	Math Achievement Data

Appendix P

Student Name	Attendance Data (Before Monitoring Program)	Literacy Achievement Data (Before Monitoring Program)	Math Achievement Data (Before Monitoring Program)	Attendance Data (After Monitoring Program)	Literacy Achievement Data (After Monitoring Program)	Math Achievement Data (After Monitoring Program)

Appendix Q

	Sunday	Monday	Tuesday	Wednesday	Thursday	Friday	Saturday
Unit 2- Week #1	11/8	11/9 1 Citizenship in Ancient Times!	11/10 2 Citizenship in Ancient Times!	11/11 3 (Half Day) Purpose of Ancient Governments	11/12 4 Secondary Source Analysis	11/13 5 Purpose of Government (Secondary Source Analysis) HW #1	11/14
Unit 2- Week #2	11/15	11/16 6 Traits of Citizenship	11/17 7 Mapping Ancient Middle East	11/18 8 Ancient Civilizations	11/19 9 Map Quiz	11/20 10 (Half Day) Picture Analysis	11/21
Unit 2- Week #3	11/22	11/23 11 Warring City States	11/24 12 Primary Source Analysis HW #2	11/25 No School (Thanksgiving Break)	11/26 No School (Thanksgiving Break)	11/27 No School (Thanksgiving Break)	11/28
Unit 2- Week #4	11/29	11/30 13 Class Discussion: Choose a side in Ancient Times!	12/1 14 Class Discussion: Choose a side in Ancient Times!	12/2 15 Claim and Evidence Practice	12/3 16 Claim and Evidence Practice HW #3	12/4 17 Historical Essay Prep	12/5
Unit 2- Week #5	12/6	12/7 Science Education Field Trip (Entire 6th Grade)	12/8 Science Education Field Trip (Entire 6th Grade)	12/9 Science Education Field Trip (Entire 6th Grade)	12/10 Science Education Field Trip (Entire 6th Grade)	12/11 Science Education Field Trip (Entire 6th Grade)	12/12
Unit 2- Week #6	12/13	12/14 18 Historical Essay	12/15 19 Historical Essay	12/16 20 Historical Essay	12/17 21 Historical Essay	12/18 22 Historical Essay	12/19

Appendix R

Winter Break	12/20	12/21	12/22	12/23	12/24	12/25	12/26
	Winter Break (No School)	Winter Break (No School)	Winter Break (No School)	Winter Break (No School)	Winter Break (No School)	Winter Break (No School)	
Winter Break	12/27	12/28	12/29	12/30	12/31	1/1	1/2
	Winter Break (No School)	Winter Break (No School)	Winter Break (No School)	Winter Break (No School)	Winter Break (No School)	Winter Break (No School)	
Unit 2- Week #7	1/3	1/4	1/5	1/6	1/7	1/8	1/9
		23	24	25	26	27	
		Inventions of the Ancient World	Impact of Technology	Social Class Analysis	Social Class Analysis	Impact of War	
			HW #4				
Unit 2- Week #8	1/10	1/11	1/12	1/13	1/14	1/15	1/16
		28	29	30	31	32	
		Class Discussion: Art Analysis	Class Discussion: Art Analysis	Thesis Statement	Paragraph Activity- Thesis Statement Practice	Start of Rebellions	
Unit 2- Week #9	1/17	1/18	1/19	1/20	1/21	1/22	1/23
		No School (MLK Day)	33	34	35	36	
			Impact of Rebellions	Review Day	Test	Review Common Errors on Test	
Unit 2- Week #10	1/24	1/25	1/26	1/27	1/28	1/29	1/30
		37	38	39	40	41	
		Webquest	Webquest	Article Analysis	Article Analysis	(Half Day) Newspaper Article	

Appendix S

Date: Tuesday, September 9, 2020

Do Now: Write down your homework and then start the warm up

Homework: Ancient Civilization Reading and Questions: DD- 9/11, DL: 9/18

Objective: SWBAT: describe the 8 themes of geography

Agenda: Warm Up -> Close Read -> 8 Themes of Geography Reading/Questions -> Interactive Exit Ticket

Appendix T

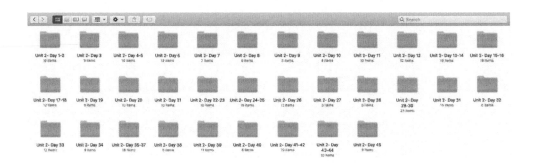

Appendix U

Sample Lesson Plan: Sixth Grade Social Studies

Teacher: Mr. Katzel	Grade/Subject: 6th Grade Social Studies	Unit/Day of Unit: Unit 1, Day 2
Periods: 1,2,3,6	Previous Learning: Analyzed maps of Europe, Online mapping activities	State Standard human and physical characteristics by analyzing maps
Academic Vocabulary: Human Geography, Physical Geography, Human Characteristics, Physical Characteristics	Daily Objective: SWBAT (Students Will Be Able To) – Identify human and physical characteristics by analyzing maps and other secondary sources	Essential Questions: Why do maps change?
Warm Up/Introduction: Analyze a Map Worksheet	Exit Ticket/Summarization: On the classroom portal, there will be a multiple choice exit car	Lesson Timing (Estimation in Minutes) 1. Warm Up (5) 2. Geography Close Read (5) 3. Map Analysis (15) 4. Secondary Source Analysis (15) 5. Review Secondary Source Analysis (5) 6. Exit Card (15)

Appendix V

Teacher: Mr. Katzel, Sixth Grade Team Leader & Social Studies	**Email: step hen.X.XXX xxx@_____ ___.com**	**School Phone: 209-XXX-xxxx**	**Student Name:** John Doe	**OI Grade:** 92% *(A)* Formative Grade Percentage – 90% Summative Grade Percentage –
				95% Homework Grade Percentage- 100% Essay Grade Percentage – 90%
Strengths 1. Asks for help/ clarification 2. Comes to class on time 3. Comes prepared with materials	**Area(s) to Discuss** 1. Turning in homework on time	**Action Steps for Success** 1. Weekly check-in from Mr. Katzel by email 2. Check assignments on the online portal	**Action Steps for Success** 3. Write down the homework each day in the student planner	**Notes:**